A Shared Experience and Nottingham Playhouse Theatre Company
co-production

World Premiere

Mermaid

by **Polly Teale**

SHARED EXPERIENCE

Shared Experience has pioneered a thrillingly distinctive performance style that celebrates the union of physical and text-based theatre.

The company is committed to creating work that goes beyond our everyday lives, taking flight into the imagination and examining the hidden parts of the self. Tackling potent universal themes, Shared Experience explores the relationship between the world we inhabit and our inner lives.

Like most other arts organisations we need to look for funding from every source to ensure that we thrive and grow. You can help us build on our ambition to produce bold, innovative and accessible theatre, please visit our website to find out how you can support us.

'Pushing the boat of theatricality way beyond its usual moorings'

The Guardian on Shared Experience

f /SharedExperience **𝕏** @setheatre #Mermaid
sharedexperience.org.uk
Shared Experience, Oxford Playhouse, Beaumont Street,
Oxford OX1 2LW   T: 01865 305301

Shared Experience is the resident company at Oxford Playhouse.
For more information visit **www.oxfordplayhouse.com**

Andrew Lloyd Webber
Foundation

Supported using public funding by
ARTS COUNCIL ENGLAND
LOTTERY FUNDED

The Andrew Lloyd Webber Foundation is delighted to support the posts of Associate Producer and Director for 3 years at Shared Experience. The Foundation welcomes the commitment of Shared Experience to nurture young talent and enrich the quality of life both for individuals and within local communities.

Finn Hanlon

A Shared Experience and Nottingham Playhouse Theatre Company co-production

Mermaid

By Polly Teale

THE COMPANY

Mermaid	Ritu Arya
Mother, Grandmer and Queen	Polly Frame
Blue	Natalie Gavin
Prince	Finn Hanlon
Mermaid	Miranda Mac Letten
King	Steve North
Mermaid	Amaka Okafor
Little Mermaid	Sarah Twomey

Other parts played by members of the company

Writer & Director	Polly Teale
Designer	Tom Piper
Choreographer & Movement Director	Liz Ranken
Lighting Designer	Oliver Fenwick
Composer & Sound Designer	Jon Nicholls
Associate Director	Laura Farnworth
Voice Coach	Majella Hurley
Costume Supervisor	Gayle Woodsend
Production Manager	Andy Bartlett & Paul Hennessy
Assistant Production Manager	Andy Hunt
Assistant Lighting Designer	Will Evans
Company Stage Manager	Emma Hansford
Deputy Stage Manager	Lauren Harvey
Assistant Stage Manager	Sarah Barnes
Wardrobe Manager	Aly Fielden
Casting Director	Amy Ball
Associate Producer	Hannah Groombridge
Production Photography	Kristin Perers & Robert Day

The performance will last approximately 2hrs including an interval.

First performed at Nottingham Playhouse on 13 March 2015.

Writer and Director Polly Teale talks about her fascination with *The Little Mermaid*

Can you remember first hearing the *Little Mermaid* story?

As a child I was first bewitched by the tale of *The Little Mermaid*. I had it on a record and would play it and sit and sob on the settee, much to the bewilderment of my brothers. It wasn't until years later that I found myself wondering what it was about this dark coming-of-age story, about a mermaid who had her tongue cut out, that spoke to me so powerfully.

At the centre of the story is the experience of puberty and the self-consciousness that comes with it, a sort of loss of self.

The mermaids live beneath the ocean in a state of unselfconscious freedom until they come of age and swim up to the surface to see the world above. Leaving behind the (amniotic fluid of the) ocean, the mermaid is suddenly confronted by herself as a separate entity in a vast universe. From this moment there is no going back to safety. She has glimpsed the world in all its beauty and brutality and in that same instance fallen in love with a mortal Prince. She can no longer remember what it is to feel complete within herself. For the first time in her life she experiences desire and with it comes loneliness. She must live beneath the ocean, invisible to the world of men, or else sacrifice her tongue, her voice in order to walk and try to gain the Prince's love. She is warned that every step she takes she will feel like she is walking on knives.

It seems that even my ten-year-old self understood that there was something in this impossible choice that I could recognise. As a girl I sensed that, to leave behind childhood was to risk losing the freedom to exist on your own terms, to sacrifice your voice in order to try to please others, to gain their approval and love. The mermaid's sacrifice, her reliance on her physical beauty to win the Prince, expressed an uncomfortable reality. Whatever I might be inside it was what I looked like that determined my value.

Do you think that is particularly true today with so much advertising and imagery everywhere we look?

In an age of mass media, of Facebook, Instagram and Snapchat, we are constantly looking at our own reflections and at idealised images of others. We spend vast amounts of money on beauty products. Dieting is an obsession and use of plastic surgery has quadrupled in ten years. Fifty thousand women had invasive procedures in Britain last year. Removing body hair has become the norm. It feels like this is a story with increasing relevance. It's not surprising that we are seeing an epidemic of self-harm amongst teenage girls. As women obsess about calories and totter around in six-inch heels to make themselves appear thinner, the mermaid's story speaks of the extreme lengths that women will go to alter themselves to win approval and of the crippling self-consciousness that can characterise modern life.

That's not to say that we shouldn't enjoy styling and decorating ourselves. That is an innate human instinct that we see in all humans, even in tribes in remote places who have no access to mirrors. It can be a source of pleasure and creativity if it is not based in a sense of lack, of inadequacy.

Do the mermaids know what they look like?

No they don't. It is strange to think that it is only relatively recently that ordinary people have had access to mirrors. I often wonder how it would alter our sense of self if we had no idea how we appeared to others. I decided that in the world beneath the ocean there were no mirrors, that the mermaids would not know what they looked like. They would be unselfconsciously curious, like very young children or animals, living inside their bodies looking out at the world, not watching themselves with a critical gaze. It is not until they witness the world above that they understand themselves to be separate beings who are visible to others. With this understanding comes self-consciousness and the knowledge of our essential aloneness, of death, of anxiety, of need and desire. In my version of the story the mermaids are immortal. Beneath the ocean there is no time.

Would you say that in the play we are looking at our human world through the eyes of the mermaids?

Yes. I wanted to see our world through their eyes in all its strangeness. To see the arbitrary hierarchies that exist, how simply by accident of birth some lives are given great importance whilst others are completely expendable. I wanted to see the bizarre nature of royalty and its archaic sexism whereby princes are sent to war whilst princesses are dressed up in expensive clothes to receive bouquets of flowers and wave at crowds of admirers. Few of us have ever heard Kate Middleton speak and yet we see millions of photographs of her and read endless column inches about her outfits. I wanted to see through the eyes of the mermaids our obsession with a certain artificial, narrow idea of beauty, to see the power of the media to distort and shape our sense of self.

Tell us about the decision to involve teenage girls in the production.

Our production will involve a chorus of young women recruited in each city on tour who will create the sound of the mermaids singing. They will also take part in a nationwide project that accompanies the show that looks at the effect of the media on girls' sense of self and empowers them to challenge myths about femininity. Onstage the mermaid chorus will bear witness as a girl faces the challenge of becoming a young woman in a complex world.

The play begins very much in our contemporary world. There is a sense of recession, of a family struggling to cope. Was it important to you to enter the story through a modern teenager?

Yes, I wanted to avoid it feeling like a twee middle-class story about a girl who reads fairy tales. At the beginning of the play we see how a teenager is ostracised because she is still, at thirteen, playing imaginary games. She lives by the sea and loves to swim and is fascinated by mermaids, imagining that they exist and can speak to her. I wanted to explore the pressure on young women to grow up quickly and abandon play, becoming preoccupied by appearance, judging one another and seeing one another as competitors. Her father has been made redundant and so she can't afford the branded products her classmates are wearing. Whilst her erstwhile friends are all at a party having a makeover she sits alone staring at the screen seeking escape. When instead a nasty video message appears from her classmates she turns to her favourite fairy story of *The Little Mermaid* for answers. Diving down into the world of the story we watch her as real life starts to entwine with that of the mermaids.

Ritu Arya, Miranda Mac Letten, Steve North, Amaka Okafor, Sarah Twomey, Finn Hanlon

'Of all the animals on earth man alone knows that he must die. And so he longs to cheat death, to forget his mortality. He builds and he buys and he conquers. He tries to believe, to have faith. He snatches at pleasure. Gorges himself on whatever scraps he can find. But all the time he knows that his hour is coming. That soon he will be foam on the ocean.'

Miranda Mac Letten

Amaka Okafor

Natalie Gavin and Sarah Twomey

Finn Hanlon

'She saw in his gaze a shifting sea of questions. She saw longing and fear and tenderness. She saw astonishing beauty, like moonlight on water, and she saw the depths of his loneliness.'

Ritu Arya

An extract from *Once Upon a Time.*
A short history of Fairy Tale

by Marina Warner

Like a mother tongue, fairy stories become part of our mental furniture.

But a fairy tale doesn't exist in a fixed form or medium; it's something like a tune that can migrate from a symphony to a penny whistle. Or you can compare it to a plant genus, to roses or fungi or grasses which can seed and root and flower here and there, changing species and colour and size and shape where they spring. The language of fairy tale is fluid and shape-shifting.

But when I allude to *'The Little Mermaid'* or to *'Bluebeard'*, you know where we are. This state of knowingness excites a desire to know more and know it differently, to detect the deeper meaning behind the tale, that 'the meaning of one thing could also be the meaning of a greater thing.' A consequence of this has been a spate of anti-tales and counter-tales, inversions and twists, in which writers or film and theatre makers enter the well-known story from a new angle in order to refresh it.

Fairy tales began to grow up and address adults again, in the late 70s with Angela Carter's *The Bloody Chamber*. No longer children's fare, the tales were opened up to reveal their harsh, unflinchingly realist inner core, through the renderings of a fellowship of writers. The writers – chiefly but not only female – were demanding that women have a voice in the stories, and they are still putting new wine in old bottles, in Carter's phrase, to watch them explode.

With this change of intended audience, fairy tales have lost the innocence that Dickens praised in them so trustingly. Hollywood may want to forget villainy but elsewhere, their dreams are no longer rainbow-coloured, their wishful thinking no longer starry-eyed. 'The reign of fairy tales … could be ecstasy,' the Italian writer Cristina Campo has noted, 'but it is above all a land of pathos, of symbols of pain.'

Some of the writers and artists who are wrapping fairy tales in darkness are keeping to the spirit of the form as a truth-telling conduit, dislike of shallow promises and easy solutions in times of savage acts of war, eco-disasters, child abuse, and so many other horrors, have grounded fairy tale; the escapist stories have changed and become lenses through which hard truths are inspected.

Once Upon A Time is published by OUP

Polly Frame, Amaka Okafor and Ritu Arya

Finn Hanlon, Steve North and Polly Frame

Sarah Twomey and Finn Hanlon

CAST

Ritu Arya
Mermaid

Theatre credits include: *The Fourth Wise Man; The Collector* (Gilded Balloon/Arcola Theatre); *As You Like It* (Transport Theatre); *Carpe Diem* (National Theatre); *Liar Liar* (Unicorn Theatre); *1001 Nights* (Transport/Unicorn Theatre).

Television and Film credits include: *Sherlock 3: Sign of Three, The Tunnel* and *Doctors*.

Polly Frame
Mother, Grandmer & Queen

Theatre credits include: *Arcadia* (Tobacco Factory); *Twelfth Night* (Filter Theatre); *Pastoral* (Soho Theatre); *After Miss Julie* (Young Vic); *The Crossing 66 Books* (Bush Theatre); *The Comedy Of Errors* (Stafford Shakespeare Festival); *Earthquakes in London* (National Theatre); *The Count of Monte Cristo* (West Yorkshire Playhouse); *Macbeth* (Chichester Festival, West End and Broadway); *Home-Work* (Bodies in Flight for Singapore Esplanade); *A Response to Twelfth Night* (Filter Theatre); *The Prime of Miss Jean Brodie, Poor Mrs Pepys* (New Vic); *ACDC* (Royal Court); *Cleansed* (Arcola); *Who By Fire, Skinworks* (Bodies in Flight); *Seven and a Half Minutes of Happiness, Di-sect, Eve* (Bristol Old Vic).

Television credits include: *Man Down, The Tunnel, Coronation Street, Holby City, Doctors, The Curse of the Hope Diamond, Silent Witness, EastEnders, Bunny Town, Sea of Souls, Accused, Life Begins, New Tricks, Meet the Magoons, The Giblets* and *Servants*.

Film credits include: *Macbeth, Half Light* and *Duplicity*.

Natalie Gavin
Blue

Theatre credits include: *The Crucible*, directed by Yäel Farber (Old Vic); *Bracken Moor* (Shared Experience).

Television credits include: *Prisoners Wives, The Syndicate* and *Shameless*.

Film credits include: Young Andrea Dunbar in *The Arbor; Hector; Jasmine* and *The Knife That Killed Me*.

Radio credits include: *Who Cares?* (BBC Radio 4).

Finn Hanlon
Prince

Theatre credits include: *War Horse* (National Theatre Tour); *A Midsummer Night's Dream, Twelth Night, The Taming of the Shrew, Henry V, The Winter's Tale* (Propeller); *The Trial* (Watford Palace Theatre); *Private Peaceful* (National Tour); *The Scarecrow and his Servant* (Southwark Playhouse); *Beautiful Thing* (BAC); *Once We Were Mothers* (Orange Tree Theatre); *Iron Eyelashes* (Imaginary Forces); *Road* (Broadway Theatre); *Alice Through the Looking Glass* (2K); *Romeo and Juliet* (New Wolsey Theatre); *Tartuffe* (Bristol Old Vic); *Tesco Children's Festival* (K'Lamity); *Blue Remembered Hills, Merrily We Roll Along* (Sherman Cymru); *'Tis Pity She's a Whore* (Bristol Old Vic).

Television and Film credits include: *Being Human, Joiner Video, Tristan and Isolde* and *Not Me.*

Miranda Mac Letten
Mermaid

Miranda Mac Letten has a First Class Honours Degree from London Contemporary Dance School. After graduating she became an apprentice for Punchdrunk and the English National Opera's *The Duchess of Malfi*. She has continued performing professionally in *The Drowned Man: A Hollywood Fable*, the biggest and most ambitious production yet from the award-winning Punchdrunk.

Site Specific and Immersive Theatre has featured heavily in Miranda's career, going on to be part of Bold Tendencies *Titus Andronicus,* a collaboration with Parkour practitioners, beat boxers and actors.

Other companies she has worked with include Secret Cinema, Smallpetitklein, Gideon Reeling, C-12 Dance Theatre, The People Pile and Bicycle Ballet. She is founder of her own company Kerfuffle Dance.

'Up above there is one thing that is prized above all others, that is more precious than life itself. One thing for which man will sacrifice all. A drug he cannot resist. You have never seen yourself in a mirror but when you do you will see that you possess the greatest prize of all.'

Steve North
King

Theatre credits include: *Down By The Greenwood Side* (Brighton Festival); *War Horse* (National Theatre/West End); *Great Expectations* (Beckmann Unicorn); *Kemble's Riot* (Pleasance/Riverside); *Brighton 'Til I Die* (Fuel/Brighton Theatre Royal); *Meeting Joe Strummer* (Edinburgh Fringe First Winner and National Tours); *Pretend You Have Big Buildings* (Royal Exchange, Manchester); *Not The Love I Cry For* (Arcola Theatre); *Red All Over* (Paddock Theatre Co); *Fever Pitch* (Arts Theatre & National Tour - nominated for Best Actor in the Manchester Evening News Awards); *The Football Factory* (National Tour); *Pretty Vacant* (Croydon Warehouse).

Television and film credits include: *War Horse NT Live, Closed Circuit, South West Nine, Holby City, Doctors, Doctor Who: A Christmas Carol, Mongrels, EastEnders, The Bill, Whistleblower, The Day Britain Stopped, Casualty, Midsomer Murders, Sense & Sensibility, Murphy's Law, Vital Signs, Woof, Is Harry On The Boat?* and *London's Burning.*

Amaka Okafor
Mermaid

Theatre credits include: *Bird* (Derby Theatre and Tour); *Glasgow Girls, The Bacchae* (National Theatre of Scotland); *Dr Korczak's Example* (Manchester Royal Exchange/Arcola); *Flathampton* (Theatre Royal Nottingham and Royal & Derngate Theatre); *Sabbat* (Dukes Theatre Lancaster); *The Snow Queen, The Three Musketeers, Beauty and the Beast, The Garbage King, The Tempest, The London Eye Mystery, Cinderella* (Unicorn Theatre); *Branded* (Old Vic); *Robin Hood, Babe's in the Wood, When Brecht Met Stanislavski* (Salisbury Playhouse); *Meantime* (Soho Theatre); *Ya get me?* (Old Vic productions); *Tracy Beaker Gets Real!* (Nottingham Playhouse/ National Tour); *Stamping, Shouting and Singing Home* (Polka Theatre Company); *Red Oleander* (Myriad Productions).

Television includes: *Grandpa in my Pocket, Doctors* and *The Bill.*

Sarah Twomey
Little Mermaid

Sarah Twomey makes her professional theatre debut in *Mermaid*.

Theatre credits at RADA include: *There and Back, The Five Wives of Maurice Pinder, The Lady from the Sea, Niggles* and *The Sea.*

CREATIVES

Polly Teale
Writer & Director

Polly Teale has created a unique body of work as a writer and director that has won critical and audience acclaim with productions transferring to the West End and touring internationally. An award-winning theatre practitioner, she has been artistic director of Shared Experience since 1995. She has also written a number of original plays and stage adaptations, including *Jane Eyre* and *Brontë*, and *After Mrs Rochester* for which she won the Evening Standard Award for Best Director and the Time Out Award for Best West End Production.

Other directing credits include: *Bracken Moor, Mary Shelley, Speechless* (co-writer/director), *The Glass Menagerie, Mine* (writer/director), *Ten Tiny Toes, Kindertransport, Madame Bovary, The Clearing, A Doll's House, The House of Bernarda Alba, Desire Under the Elms,* and, as co-director, *War and Peace* and *The Mill on the Floss.*

Last year Polly directed *Bakersfield Mist* in the West End. She is the director of the feature film of *Brontë*, which is currently in development.

Tom Piper
Designer

Tom Piper was the Associate Designer of the Royal Shakespeare Company for ten years. Recent work there includes: *The Christmas Truce; Antony & Cleopatra* (RSC/Miami/New York); *Boris Godunov; Much Ado About Nothing; Macbeth; City Madam* and *Histories Cycle* for which he won the 2009 Olivier Award for Best Costume Design and was nominated for the 2009 Olivier Award for Best Set Design (Courtyard Theatre and the Roundhouse); *As You Like It; The Grain Store; The Drunks.*

Other recent designs include: *Hamlet; Libertine; King Lear* (Citizens Theatre, Glasgow); *Bakersfield Mist* (West End); *Red Velvet* (Tricycle Theatre and New York); *Bracken Moor* (Shared Experience and Tricycle Theatre); *The House that will not Stand* (Tricycle Theatre); *Goodbye To All That; Vera, Vera, Vera* (Royal Court Theatre and Theatre Local); *Richard III; The Tempest; As You Like It* (Bridge Project at BAM and the Old Vic); *Dealer's Choice* (Menier Chocolate Factory and West End); *Plough And The Stars; The Crucible; Six Characters In Search Of An Author* (Abbey, Dublin); *The Big Meal* (Bath Unistov); *The King's Speech* (Birmingham & Tour); *Tamburiaine* (TFANA New York).

Tom was the Designer for the acclaimed installation, *Blood Swept Lands and Seas of Red* at the Tower of London with ceramic artist Paul Cummins.

Liz Ranken
Choreographer & Movement Director

Credits this year include: Movement Director and Choreographer for *Orpheo* at the Round House produced with the Royal Opera House.

For her own productions she has won The Place Portfolio Award and Capital Award (Edinburgh). She won a Time-Out award for bringing theatre alive with movement. She was a Core Member of DV8 Physical Theatre.

Liz paints professionally, and has a painting in The Heinz Archive at The National Portrait Gallery and in The Portrait Collection at The Royal Shakespeare Company (RSC). She is an Associate Artist of the RSC and has worked there extensively as a Movement Director (Histories Cycle, Complete Works).

In Scotland she has performed with Cat A Theatre Company, touring prisons and theatres and performed in site specific work with NVA.

She is an Associate Artist of Shared Experience.

Oliver Fenwick
Lighting Designer

Theatre credits include: *Bracken Moor* (Shared Experience); *Love's Labour's Lost; Much Ado About Nothing; Wendy and Peter Pan; The Winter's Tale; The Drunks; The Grain Store; Julius Caesar* (RSC); *Hobson's Choice; The Beggar's Opera (Open Air Theatre); The Big Meal; Thérèse Raquin* (TRB); *Bakersfield Mist* (Duchess Theatre, London); *Into the Woods; Sunday in the Park with George* (Théâtre du Châtelet); Belfast); *Red Velvet* (Tricycle Theatre & St Ann's Warehouse New York); *Godchild; Private Lives; The Giant; Glass Eels; Comfort Me with Restoration* (Hampstead Theatre); *Routes* (Royal Court); *Handbagged; A Boy and His Soul; Paper Dolls* (Tricycle Theatre); *King Lear; Candida* (Theatre Royal Bath); *To Kill a Mockingbird* (Open Air Theatre & UK Tour); *Werther* (Scottish Opera); *Bernice* (Donmar Warehouse); *Blue/Orange* (Theatre Royal Brighton, UK Tour); *The Witness* (Royal Court); *After Ms Julie* (Young Vic); *The Madness of George III* (Theatre Royal Bath & West End); *The Kitchen Sink; If There Is I Haven't Found it Yet; The Contingency Plan* (Bush Theatre); *My City; Ruined* (Almeida Theatre); *Saved* (Lyric Hammersmith); *Huis Clos* (Trafalgar Studios, Donmar); *Realism & Mongrel Island* (Soho Theatre); *'Tis Pity She's A Whore; Hay Fever; A Doll's House* (West Yorkshire Playhouse), *The Holy Rosenburgs; Happy Now* (National Theatre); *The Winter's Tale* (Guthrie Theatre USA); *Much Ado About Nothing; Mary Stuart* (Sweden); *A Number* (Menier Chocolate Factory); *The Picture* (Salisbury Playhouse); *The Merry Widow* (Opera North); *Hamlet* (Sheffield); *Disconnect* (Royal Court); *Ghosts* (Duchess Theatre - Thelma Holt Productions); *The Line* (Arcola); *Sunshine Over Leith* (Dundee Rep and tour); *Mary Poppins* (UK tour); *Endgame* (Liverpool Everyman); *Hedda Gabler; The Chairs* (Gate Theatre); *The Lady from the Sea;*

She Stoops to Conquer (Birmingham Rep); *Terms of Endearment* (tour); *Kean* (Apollo, Bristol Old Vic and tour); *Henry V; Mirandolina; A Conversation* (Royal Exchange); *My Fair Lady* (Cameron Mackintosh/NT tour); *The Elephant Man; The Caretaker; The Comedy of Errors; Bird Calls; Iphigenia* (Crucible, Sheffield); *The Solid Gold Cadillac* (Garrick Theatre); *The Secret Rapture* (Lyric Theatre); *Noises Off; All My Sons; Dr Faustus* (Liverpool Playhouse); *On the Piste* (Birmingham Rep).

Opera credits include: *Electra* (Sweden); *The Merry Widow* (Opera Australia); *Samson et Delilah; Lohengrin* (Royal Opera House); *The Trojan Trilogy; The Nose* (Royal Opera House Linbury Studio); *The Gentle Giant* (Royal Opera House Clore Studio); *The Threepenny Opera* (Opera Group); *L'opera Seria* (Batignano Festival).

Jon Nicholls
Composer / Sound Designer

Jon Nicholls studied composition at London College of Music and electroacoustic music at Dartington.

Music/sound scores for theatre include: *Spring Storm; Beyond The Horizon; The Holy Rosenbergs* (National Theatre); *Bakersfield Mist* (Duchess); *Bracken Moor* (Shared Experience); *Who's Afraid of Virginia Woolf?* (Sheffield Crucible); *Yerma; Idomeneus* (Gate); *The Norman Conquests* (Liverpool Playhouse); *Play Strindberg; Things We Do For Love; Intimate Apparel; In The Next Room; Red Light Winter; The Welsh Boy; Deadkidsongs; The Double; Spanish Golden Age season* (Theatre Royal Bath); *Merlin; The Wind In The Willows; Dancing at Lughnasa; A Midsummer Night's Dream; Eden End; Humble Boy; The Prime of Miss Jean Brodie; In Praise of Love; Young America season* (Northampton); *Blue Remembered Hills; Art; The Changeling; Silas Marner* (Theatr Clwyd); *Rutherford and Son* (Northern Stage); *Katherine DeSouza; The Mothership; Linda* (Birmingham Rep); *Amadeus; Masterclass; Be My Baby* (Derby Playhouse); *Private Lives; Much Ado About Nothing; If I Were You; Rosencrantz and Guildenstern Are Dead; Arcadia; The Heretic; The Seagull* (Library Theatre, Manchester); *The Picture* (Salisbury Playhouse).

Screen work includes: scores for numerous documentaries for the BBC, ITV, Channel 4 and Sky, and over 30 short films.

Extensive music and sound design for BBC Radio Drama includes: *Earthsea; Five Fever Tales; The Broken Word; Pink Mist; Erebus; Laurels and Donkeys; In Memoriam; At The Mountains of Madness; The Shadow Over Innsmouth; Between Friends; Babel's Tower; Faust; Cat on a Hot Tin Roof; Caesar Price Our Lord; It's Better with Animals; The Histories of Herodotus; The Time Machine; Zen and The Art of Motorcycle Maintenance; What I Heard About Iraq* (Prix Italia Jury Special Mention).

Jon has composed two operas: *Falling Across* and *Flicker* which was recently premiered at Sadlers Wells.

Laura Farnworth
Associate Director

Laura Farnworth is Artistic Director of Undercurrent, currently developing *Meet George*, premiering at Camden People's Theatre in autumn 2015.

As Director: *Mother and Child* (R&D - Young Vic); *Our Style is Legendary* (Tristan Bates / Nottingham Playhouse); *Dying* (R&D – ATC / The Gate); *Abel Sanchez; Just so Stories* (STK); *A Little Music* (Ignition Festival, Tristan Bates); *Flygirl* (National Studio); *Floor 44; Trickster* (ATC / Young Vic); *Jungle* (BAC / Camden People's Theatre / Theatre Royal Bath); *The King of Schnorrers* (Camden People's Theatre); *Don Q* (Edinburgh Festival).

As Co-Director: with State of Flux, Oxford Samuel Beckett Trust Award 2013: *The Finalists*.

As Assistant Director: *Public Enemy* (Young Vic); *My City* (Almeida); *Happy Now?* (National Theatre); *Moon on a Rainbow Shawl* (Royal Court).

As Dramaturg: *House on the Edge* (DanceEast); *A Study of Who* (State of Flux); *Where I Go* (National Studio); *IGNIS* (Print Room).

Laura was resident at Young Vic as part of Jerwood Assistant Directors Programme in 2013; Finalist - Genesis Directors Award 2013; Finalist - Jerwood Directors Award 2009; Finalist - Cohen Bursary. She won NSDF Award for Storytelling and attended the National Studio Directors Course.

Majella Hurley
Voice Coach

Theatre credits include: *Bracken Moor; Speechless; Jane Eyre; War and Peace; A Passage To India; After Mrs Rochester; The Brontes* (Shared Experience); *City of Angels; Fathers and Sons; Coriolanus; Days of Wine and Roses* (Donmar); *The Kitchen; Anything Goes; The Seafarer; Exiles; The Night Season* (National Theatre); *Love's Labour's Lost; A Midsummer Night's Dream* (Royal Shakespeare Company); *The Force of Change; Disconnect; Sucker Punch; Loyal Women; The Weir* (Royal Court); *Handbagged; Jerusalem; Abigail's Party; Our Boys; Journey's End; Wicked; Chicago; Some Girls; The Ladykillers; Jeeves and Wooster* (West End); *Journey's End, Pygmalion* (Broadway); *Ragtime; Hello Dolly; To Kill A Mockingbird* (Regent's Park); *The Beauty Queen of Leenane; Bingo* (Young Vic); *Ruined; Before the Party; My City* (Almeida Theatre); *The Great Game; The Bloody Sunday Inquiry; Guantanamo* (Tricycle Theatre); *A 1000 Stars, Punk Rock; Twisted Tales* (Lyric Theatre); *Sweeney Todd* (Sheffield/ ENT/Rose); *Translations* (Chichester Festival).

Television credits include: *White Girl; Cranford I & II; Little Dorrit; Wuthering Heights; Game of Thrones 3; Case Histories; Stella; Vera; State of Play; Hearts and Bones.*

Film credits include: *A Monster Calls; Toast; Intermission; Endgame; Skydance; With or Without You.*

Miranda Mac Letten, Amaka Okafor, Sarah Twomey, Ritu Arya, Polly Frame

Natalie Gavin

SHARED EXPERIENCE

Thanks to

Arts Council England.
Andrew Lloyd Webber Foundation.
Nottingham Playhouse.

Eden Rickson, Pia Ashberry, Rosie Banham, Nica Burns, Louise Chantal,
Michelle Dickson, Erin Macdonald, Tanya Rhonda, Mary Roscoe, Gemma Rowan,
Michelle Walker, Chichester Festival Theatre and all the staff at Oxford Playhouse.

The actors who worked on the research and development: Kristin Atherton,
Laure Bachelot, Audrey Brisson, Adam Burton, Cath Duggan, Anna Finkel, Natalie Gavin,
Dave Newman, Eve Ponsonby, Alex Robertson, Sophie Russell and Sam Swainsbury.

The girls who helped on the research and development: Freya Allen, Ellie Bickell,
Isobel Brook, Calypso Bressan, Saskia Cookson, Hannah Darch, Elysia Fowler
and Olivia Matterson.

All the Mermaid choruses.

Lighting hires supplied by White Light. Sound hires supplied by Stage Sound Service.
Production transport by Paul Mathew Transport.

For Shared Experience

Artistic Director	Polly Teale
Producer	Conrad Lynch
Finance Manager	Graeme Everist
Assistant Producer	Hannah Bevan
Marketing	Kate Walker for Team
Digital Marketing	Lisa Sullivan
Press	Julia Hallawell for Kate Morley PR

Board of Directors: Richard Humphreys (Chair), Olga Edridge, Caroline Jones, Alastair Petrie, Alan Rivett, Mary Roscoe

Guardian Angels: Joan Bakewell, Nica Burns, Nancy Meckler

Mermaid tour, Spring 2015

Nottingham Playhouse	13 – 21 March
West Yorkshire Playhouse, Leeds	25 – 28 March
Clwyd Theatr Cymru, Mold	31 March – 4 April
Richmond Theatre	7 – 11 April
Sherman Cymru, Cardiff	21 – 25 April
Nuffield Theatre, Southampton	28 April – 2 May
Traverse Theatre, Edinburgh	6 – 9 May
Watford Palace Theatre	12 – 16 May
Oxford Playhouse	19 – 23 May

NOTTINGHAM PLAYHOUSE
Co-Producer

Nottingham Playhouse has been one of the United Kingdom's leading producing theatres since our foundation in 1948. We welcome over 110,000 customers through our doors each year and create productions large and small: timeless classics, enthralling family shows and adventurous new commissions, often touring work nationally and internationally.

2013 marked our 50th anniversary in our current home. During those 50 years the Playhouse stage has played host to many outstanding performers and helped create a generation of dedicated theatregoers. Recent notable productions include **1984**, Steven Berkoff's **Oedipus**, Brecht and Weill's **The Threepenny Opera** and **The Kite Runner**.

★ ★ ★ ★
'Outstanding'
The Daily Mail on
The Kite Runner

★ ★ ★ ★
'An absolute delight'
The Stage on
Sleeping Beauty

★ ★ ★ ★
'Exhilarating'
The Sunday Times on
The Threepenny Opera

★ ★ ★ ★ ★
'Brilliant'
The Guardian on **1984**

To find out more about our work please see
nottinghamplayhouse.co.uk or call **0115 941 9419**

Artistic Director **Giles Croft** Chief Executive **Stephanie Sirr**

ARTS COUNCIL
ENGLAND
LOTTERY FUNDED
Supported using public funding by

Nottingham
City Council

NottinghamPlayhouse @NottmPlayhouse

Polly Teale

MERMAID

based on the book by
Hans Christian Andersen

NICK HERN BOOKS
www.nickhernbooks.co.uk

SHARED EXPERIENCE
www.sharedexperience.org.uk

Mermaid was first performed in a co-production between Shared Experience and Nottingham Playhouse at Nottingham Playhouse on 13 March 2015. The cast was as follows:

MERMAID	Ritu Arya
MOTHER/GRANDMER/QUEEN	Polly Frame
BLUE	Natalie Gavin
PRINCE	Finn Hanlon
MERMAID	Miranda Mac Letten
KING	Steve North
MERMAID	Amaka Okafor
LITTLE MERMAID	Sarah Twomey

Other parts played by members of the company

Director	Polly Teale
Designer	Tom Piper
Choreographer & Movement Director	Liz Ranken
Lighting Designer	Oliver Fenwick
Composer & Sound Designer	Jon Nicholls
Associate Director	Laura Farnworth
Voice Coach	Majella Hurley

The production subsequently toured to West Yorkshire Playhouse, Leeds; Clwyd Theatr Cymru, Mold; Richmond Theatre; Sherman Cymru, Cardiff; Nuffield Theatre, Southampton; Traverse Theatre, Edinburgh; Watford Palace Theatre and Oxford Playhouse.

For Eden

Characters

BLUE
MOTHER
ELLA
JADE
JOE
KATIE BAXTER
GRANDMER
LITTLE MERMAID
MERMAID ONE
MERMAID TWO
MERMAID THREE
FISHERMAN
MAN
KING
PRINCE
FATHER
NEWS REPORTER
PRIVATE SECRETARY
QUEEN
CHILD ONE
CHILD TWO
CHILD THREE
SECURITY GUARD
SEA WITCH

And FISHERMEN, SOLDIERS, PARAMEDICS, PALACE STAFF, JOURNALISTS, PHOTOGRAPHERS, LADIES-IN-WAITING, PROTESTERS, ROYAL GUESTS, VARIOUS ATTENDANTS

Author's Note

All other characters are played by members of the company.

The mermaids are dressed in slips and undergarments. There are no tails, only movements that suggest they are moving in water.

The Sea Witch is played by four women conjoined into one.

When the mermaids first break the surface of the ocean and see the world above, they plunge their heads into buckets of water and come up soaking. Until that moment they are dry.

The play was first performed with a choir of teenage girls in each city on tour. The girls also played guests at Katie Baxter's party and sat on stage throughout the play, joining in with the mermaids to create the sound of their unearthly singing.

The original set had a raised platform beneath which the mermaids could swim. There was a wardrobe, bed and a chair and table, which were washed away into the sea during the storm. The wardrobe hung in mid-air for the rest of the show as if floating.

Blue is always on stage and always visible as our narrator who is imagining and writing into being everything we see. She can speak words with characters or speak occasional sentences as feels right.

In the stage directions I have offered examples of how we realised the script in the original production, but these should not be taken as prescriptive. Feel free to find your own solutions.

P.T.

ACT ONE

A room in a house in a run-down seaside town in a remote part of England. Thirteen-year-old BLUE *and her family have an alternative, new-age/grunge look to them.* BLUE*'s bedroom is decorated with a collage of pictures of mermaids and mythical sea creatures.*

The sound of gulls outside.

BLUE *sits on the floor surrounded by dropped clothes. She has her phone open and is scanning Facebook and Instagram. She continues to stare at the screen throughout the conversation. Her* MOTHER *stands in the door carrying the washing basket in her arms. During the scene she picks up clothes from the bedroom floor.*

MOTHER. Have you finished that homework?

    Silence.

    I like that idea, a new version of a fairy story. You let me read it when you're done? I can guess which one it'll be.

    Silence.

    Did you hear what I said? When you've done we can watch *Bake Off*. I've made some flapjacks.

BLUE. I'm busy.

MOTHER. What you doing?

BLUE. What's it look like?

    Pause.

MOTHER. You going to see Jade at the weekend?

BLUE. Don't think so.

MOTHER. Or Ella?

BLUE. No.

MOTHER. Haven't seen her in ages. Why don't you invite them over? Have a sleepover. You can have a fire on the beach. Sausages.

BLUE. No thanks.

MOTHER. I'll get that ice cream you like.

BLUE. I said no thanks.

MOTHER. Camp out in the back like you used to.

BLUE. Are you deaf?

Beat.

MOTHER. There was no need for that.

BLUE. Or just stupid.

MOTHER. That's enough.

BLUE. Is it?

MOTHER. Your father'll be home in a minute.

BLUE. And what's he gonna do about it?

MOTHER. Take away that phone, that's what.

BLUE (*under her breath*) Loser.

Beat.

MOTHER. What did you say?

BLUE. Nothing.

MOTHER. Don't you talk about your father like that. All that he's done for you.

BLUE. It's his fault.

MOTHER. What is?

BLUE. Everyone else is invited.

MOTHER. What you talking about?

BLUE. If he had a job.

MOTHER. Invited where?

BLUE. Nowhere. Forget it.

MOTHER. What's going on?

BLUE. Nothing. Just leave me alone.

MOTHER. Is he to blame for them building a Tesco down the road? Who's going to buy fresh fish from the back of his boat when they can get frozen for half the price.

BLUE. If he had a job I wouldn't be wearing trainers you bought from the charity shop –

MOTHER. They're perfectly fine. Nearly new. They were still in the box –

BLUE. That it turns out used to belong to Katie Baxter who's having a 'celebrity party' for her fourteenth birthday, whose dad's paid for a make-up artist and professional photographer and a limousine –

MOTHER. You never told me they were hers.

BLUE. Cancer Research they call me. Oxfam. Barnardo's.

MOTHER. You've nothing to be ashamed of. She should be, throwing away a brand-new pair of shoes. Poking fun at someone who hasn't had her advantages. I've a mind to ring her parents –

BLUE. NO!

MOTHER. Or *her*. Looking down her nose.

BLUE. Don't you dare.

MOTHER. You don't need Katie Baxter and her limousine party. You stick with Ella and Jade and tell her to learn some manners.

BLUE. Just shut up about it.

MOTHER. I don't suppose they're impressed by her nonsense.

BLUE. What do you know about anything?

MOTHER. I was just saying I don't suppose they think much of her / behaviour...

BLUE (*suddenly*). They're *there*. *Everybody's* there. Singing 'Happy Birthday'. (*Shows her* MOTHER *a photo on her phone*.) Jade, Ella, Cheryl, Emily.

MOTHER. I wouldn't let you out of the house dressed like that.

BLUE. Maybe *that's* why I wasn't invited.

MOTHER. Just because Ella and Jade are at the party doesn't mean they like her.

BLUE. They haven't spoken to me for a fortnight, unless you count Jade giving my swimsuit and snorkel back.

BLUE*'s phone rings.*

MOTHER. Who's that?

BLUE (*pleased*). Ella.

MOTHER. There you go!

BLUE *gestures for her* MOTHER *to leave the room. The* MOTHER *listens from the other side of the door straining to hear.*

BLUE. Hello.

As she answers her phone we see the FaceTime sequence spring to life. A party with music and dancing and flashing lights. Gathered around the camera, a collection of GIRLS *dressed up to the nines wearing high heels and make-up.* ELLA *speaks direct to the camera.*

ELLA. Hey, Blue, that boy, the surfer you've been crazy about for months, he's here at the party.

JADE (*calling*). Joe, come and meet Blue, she never stops talking about you.

JOE. Hiya, Blue.

KATIE BAXTER. Blue told Jade she saw a mermaid on the rocks off The Point. Told her she can hear her singing in a shell she keeps under her pillow.

ELLA (*giggling*). Shurrup.

KATIE BAXTER. Made up a spell to grow a fish tail, didn't she, Jade?

ELLA. Katie says you can come to the party. Have your nails done. Look. We had a makeover. Eyelashes and everything.

KATIE BAXTER. Or is her mummy putting her to bed? Is she reading her a bedtime story? Tucking her up with a mermaid song. Hey, Joe, come and give Blue a goodnight cuddle.

JOE. Show us your tits. Sorry, forgot, you haven't got any.

KATIE BAXTER. Ah, don't be like that, Joe. Make love not war, that's what you're in to, isn't it, Blue. All that weirdo hippy peace shit.

There's a big laugh and Miley Cyrus's 'Wrecking Ball' (or similar) is turned up so loud that she can no longer hear their voices. The GIRLS *are dancing.*

We become aware of BLUE*'s* MOTHER *knocking on the door and calling.* BLUE *switches off her phone but the party continues in the darkness.* BLUE *puts on her headphones and finds 'Wrecking Ball'. We hear it loud as though we are listening to it through the headphones.*

MOTHER (*trying the door handle*). What did she say? She invite you to the party? I can walk you round there if you want to go. Open the door.

BLUE *stands on her bed and starts to gyrate provocatively to Miley Cyrus. The party is still alive in* BLUE*'s imagination in slow motion. They are watching her dance, dancing along. In slow motion* KATIE BAXTER *starts to dance provocatively with* BLUE *as if they were best friends. She pulls* BLUE *down from the bed to the centre of the dance floor. She circles* BLUE *and they dance together. Throughout the sequence,* KATIE BAXTER *keeps looking back towards*

ELLA *and* JADE, *who are watching her and smirking.*
KATIE BAXTER *imitates* BLUE, *parodying her Miley*
Cyrus impersonation. The crowd start to laugh and jeer as
KATIE BAXTER *mimes vomiting behind* BLUE's *back. She*
pushes BLUE *backwards and* BLUE *realises that everyone*
is laughing at her.

BLUE *goes to the wardrobe to see herself in the mirror and*
tries to flatten a strand of hair across her forehead,
plastering it with spit or hair gel. She puts on lipstick. She
looks at herself sideways in the mirror, pushing up her
breasts and pulling in her stomach and adjusting her clothes.
She stands on her toes, trying to imagine herself in high
heels. She pouts and assesses her appearance, pulling at the
flesh on her stomach. The GIRLS *start to prod and poke at*
her stomach and pull at her clothes and hair. The taunting
escalates until it becomes a physical struggle. Pushing them
away, BLUE *throws herself down on the floor. They follow.*
She opens a school exercise book.

She opens the book and starts to write. Lights change. The
GIRLS *from the party move in slow motion as if through*
deep water as they shed their human clothing, transforming
into MERMAIDS.

BLUE. Far, far from land, where the waters are as black as the
darkest night, where no anchor can reach the bottom, live
the mermaids. It is so deep you would have to pile a
thousand shipwrecks on top of one another before one of
them stuck out above the surface. So deep that a drowned
man might drift for ever and never reach the ocean bed. So
deep that a spoon or a key or a watch could take a year,
maybe two to reach the bottom.

A shiny silver watch from the party floats, passed from
MERMAID *to* MERMAID *as it drifts down and comes to*
rest on the ocean bed. Their movements have a
weightlessness and are stirred by the currents in the water.
Their bodies are entwined. The MERMAIDS *are curious*
and unselfconscious, more like animals than people.

BLUE *returns to the book and continues to write. From this point onward she experiences the story through the youngest of the sisters, the* LITTLE MERMAID, *following everything she does as if she were an extension of herself. Everything we see is conjured up by* BLUE*'s writing. Sometimes she speaks the lines with the characters or speaks certain key words or phrases. Throughout the play she is holding her book, often writing in it.*

Every night Grandmer would tell the mermaids stories. Of all her stories the one they wanted to hear again and again was about the land above the water. There is a great fire that men call –

GRANDMER. There is a great fire that men call the 'sun', that warms your skin. There are winds that stroke you and whisper in your ear. There are waves that tickle you all over until you cry out with laughter.

She does each action as she describes it. The MERMAIDS *squirm with excitement. They all speak at once.*

LITTLE MERMAID. What is the wind made of?

MERMAID TWO. How far is the sun?

MERMAID THREE. Where do the waves go?

MERMAID ONE. What is fire?

GRANDMER. Enough. Enough. You need to rest, to dream.

LITTLE MERMAID. We're not tired…

MERMAID TWO. Finish the story.

MERMAID THREE. Please.

The eldest, MERMAID THREE, *leans on* GRANDMER*'s knee.*

GRANDMER. Ssh. Tomorrow you will come of age and can see for yourself.

BLUE *speaks the next line with the* LITTLE MERMAID.

LITTLE MERMAID. But I am the youngest. There is for ever before I come of age. How can I bear to wait for so long?

GRANDMER. Hush now. You are still a child. A baby.

LITTLE MERMAID. No I'm not –

GRANDMER. Remember, there is nowhere up on earth as beautiful as the bottom of the ocean.

LITTLE MERMAID. Tell me, Grandmer, what are *men*?

GRANDMER *nuzzles her affectionately.*

GRANDMER. To sleep.

The other MERMAIDS *lie down to sleep.*

LITTLE MERMAID (*to* MERMAID THREE). You must promise to remember everything. Every single thing.

ALL. Ssssshhhhh.

LITTLE MERMAID But I'm not tired!

GRANDMER *turns the page as the* MERMAIDS *fall to sleep. The* LITTLE MERMAID's *eyes are still open, staring up towards the sky.*

GRANDMER. Tell me. Where did you go today?

LITTLE MERMAID (*acting it out as she explains*). I swam with the seals as far as the reef and then I taunted the anemones and dared them to catch me but they couldn't of course, so I lay on the ocean bed and made patterns with my tail and sang with a whale and then rode it back as far as the wreck.

Singing stops.

GRANDMER (*stiffening*). The wreck? You're not allowed to go to the wreck.

LITTLE MERMAID Why not?

GRANDMER. You know why. It's not safe.

LITTLE MERMAID. There are strange things there, Grandmer. Things that make you wonder.

GRANDMER. It's dangerous.

LITTLE MERMAID. Wonder about their lives, their lives up above –

GRANDMER. You must promise me, promise me whatever you do never to speak to…

LITTLE MERMAID. Who?

GRANDMER. Nobody.

LITTLE MERMAID. But you said –

GRANDMER. I told you not to go to the wreck.

LITTLE MERMAID. Look what I found.

The LITTLE MERMAID *takes the shiny silver watch out from under a hiding place. She holds it to her ear. We hear the sound of ticking.*

Listen. You can hear it.

GRANDMER. Give it to me.

LITTLE MERMAID. What is it?

GRANDMER. A clock.

LITTLE MERMAID. What is it for?

GRANDMER. You have no need –

LITTLE MERMAID (*insistent*). Tell me about the land above the water. Tell me, please.

GRANDMER *stares at the watch, fascinated by its ticking hands and shiny surfaces.*

GRANDMER. Up above there is time.

LITTLE MERMAID. Time?

GRANDMER. Life does not last for ever as it does for us mermaids. From the moment man is born he knows that his hours are numbered. The clock is ticking. Measuring in hours and minutes and seconds. He lives each day not knowing which will be his last.

The LITTLE MERMAID *is fascinated by this strange object.*

LITTLE MERMAID. The 'clock' is 'ticking'.

GRANDMER (*suddenly taking the watch*). Look at me. Promise me that you will never go to the wreck again. Never.

LITTLE MERMAID. But why not?

GRANDMER. One day your time will come. You will see for yourself. Until then you stay away.

Lights change.

BLUE. The next day the first of the mermaids swam to the surface.

MERMAID THREE *is mid-story.*

MERMAID THREE. When I put my head above the water the sky was burning. I swam towards the fire but it sank into the ocean. I dived down to find it but it had disappeared. The sky went purple then black. At first I was frightened but then I saw that the darkness was full of holes where the light leaks through. I sang to the 'stars' and a great groaning ship passed by. There were men heaving nets up out of the water. The nets were full of fishes lashing and fighting and gasping for breath.

As she speaks, we hear the sound of the sea and see a FISHERMAN throwing a net into the water from BLUE's bedroom table which has become the ship. We see another FISHERMAN sharpening a huge knife. Each rhythmic movement of the knife against steel draws the MERMAIDS, who are fascinated by this first sighting of a man. The CHOIR sings.

The men had knives that glittered in the moonlight. I saw them cut off the fin of a great shark and then they flung the wounded creature back into the ocean. I watched as it flailed and the sea turned red.

LITTLE MERMAID. What are men like?

MERMAID ONE. Did they see you?

MERMAID TWO. Did they hear you?

MERMAID THREE. As I sang the wind began to whine and the water rose up and the ship started to pitch and roll.

The FISHERMEN *throw a rope into the water and the* MERMAIDS *catch it twisting and turning, dancing with excitement as the sea rises up.*

I sang to the men. Calling them to come play in the ocean. Come and dance with the waves, but the great ship carried them away into the night.

FISHERMAN (*calling*). All hands on deck. Rig the jack lines. Reef the main sail. Bear away.

The storm rages as the FISHERMEN *try to steady the vessel.*

The MERMAIDS *swim away. The* LITTLE MERMAID *looks up towards the sky through the water.*

BLUE. None of the sisters longed to see the world above as much as the youngest who had the longest to wait. At night she would stare up through the water and see the pale light of the stars.

A boat passes overhead.

LITTLE MERMAID. Sometimes a black shadow passed over and then I knew that it was a ship sailing high above with men on board with knives that glittered in the moonlight.

The men up above the water. Do they know... do they know that we're here?

GRANDMER. There are stories.

LITTLE MERMAID. Stories?

GRANDMER. Or myths, legends, depending on whether they believe them.

LITTLE MERMAID. What do you mean?

GRANDMER. Some say they have seen us but few have lived to tell the tale. Our singing brings storms. It can cause ships to crash upon the rocks, turn sailors' minds so that they leap into the water as if into the arms of a lover only to find themselves drowning.

LITTLE MERMAID. Drowning? What is drowning?

GRANDMER. Men cannot live in the ocean just as we cannot live up above.

LITTLE MERMAID. Why not?

GRANDMER. The water, it fills their lungs and suffocates them until they're dead.

LITTLE MERMAID. Dead?

GRANDMER. Gone.

LITTLE MERMAID. Where to?

GRANDMER. You remember I told you, up above there is time. Life does not last for ever as it does for us mermaids. Even if men are lucky enough to survive the many dangers, the human body, it changes, it decays as the years pass, until one day it is worn out. The life drains away and is gone. For ever.

LITTLE MERMAID. But how is that possible? Where does it go?

GRANDMER. No one knows. Some say that the human soul lives on. Some say that death is the end and then there is nothing. It is as if they become foam on the ocean.

LITTLE MERMAID. But how can they bear to live knowing that they will so soon be gone for ever? How can they bear it?

GRANDMER. They must. They have no choice.

LITTLE MERMAID. What is a 'soul', Grandmer?

GRANDMER. A soul?

LITTLE MERMAID. What is it for?

GRANDMER. Shshsh. Tell me where did you go today?

Lights change.

BLUE. As the years passed, each of the mermaids came of age and told of their experience above the water. The youngest mermaid listened to every word and remembered everything.

MERMAID TWO *is drenched with water. She is in the middle of her story.*

MERMAID TWO. The sky was blue and the sea smooth as glass glittering in the sunlight. I felt the heat on my skin, the hot still air. A battered boat drifted on the water. As I swam closer I could see that the boat was...

The image forms like 'The Raft of the Medusa', but with a hazy stillness as in intense heat. A dead man is entwined with a living. A vulture cries as he circles above. The CHOIR *sings.* MERMAID TWO *is fascinated by this ghostly apparition.*

The boat was full of men crammed together. At first I thought that they were sleeping but then I saw that their eyes were open, staring, though they did not see. Their limbs were beautiful, like the sinews in the waves.

A MAN *leans over the edge of the boat towards the* MERMAID. *He croaks a single word: 'Water!'*

Could he not see there was water everywhere...

Again the MAN *reaches and speaks: 'Water! Water!'*

The MERMAID *examines the* MAN's *strange human form, fascinated by his living flesh.*

His eyes glittered in the sunlight, his lips opened like the petals of a strange underwater flower.

What happened to you?

MAN (*slumps back*). Work, looking for work. No jobs. No food. No water. Water.

MERMAID TWO *cups her hands and fills them with sea water, offering it to the dying* MAN. *He drinks and then spits out the salty water.*

The image dissolves.

LITTLE MERMAID. Work? What is work?

GRANDMER. Up above some are born by chance into lives of privilege and plenty whilst others must struggle to survive, their lives lost to toil and hardship.

LITTLE MERMAID. What do you mean?

GRANDMER. Man must work for money to feed his children, to put a roof over his head.

LITTLE MERMAID. Money.

GRANDMER. Up above everything has its price. Down below we are lucky. Whatever we want for is ours.

Lights change.

A year later. MERMAID ONE's *coming of age. The sound of an explosion detonating. She is excited.* MERMAID ONE *becomes the fire and the sparks as she describes them.*

MERMAID ONE. As I put my head above the water the sea burst into flames. I never saw anything so beautiful. Fire danced on the waves and a thousand sparks fell into the ocean. Then great billowing clouds rose up from the water and swallowed the sky. There were strange noises as if the world was cracking apart.

MERMAID ONE *is surrounded by smoke and fire and the sound of guns.*

As the smoke cleared I saw a gigantic ship slowly sinking into the water.

Two SOLDIERS *climb to the top of the wardrobe as if clinging to a piece of debris in the water. They pray for their lives. The sound of a great wave. The* MERMAIDS *become the water dragging the* SOLDIERS *down as they struggle to keep afloat. The* SOLDIERS *are dragged from the wardrobe as if by the waves. They cling to the table, wrestling each other into the water. One of the* SOLDIERS *succeeds in pushing the other off the the table into the water.*

I told them how beautiful it is at the bottom of the ocean.

MERMAID THREE *rises up beneath the table looking into the eyes of the remaining* SOLDIER. *He is mesmerised. The* CHOIR *sings. Entranced by the* MERMAID, *he is seduced into the water as if into an ecstasy of drowning.*

The MERMAIDS *explore the drowned bodies, gently nudging and rolling them in the water, fascinated by their strange human form.*

Look what we've found, Grandmer. Look.

LITTLE MERMAID. Are they dead?

GRANDMER. They must be at war.

LITTLE MERMAID. What's war?

GRANDMER. A terrible waste of life.

MERMAID TWO. What happens?

GRANDMER. Parents lose their children and children lose their parents.

MERMAID THREE. Lose them?

GRANDMER. They're killed.

MERMAID ONE. Why?

GRANDMER. They quarrel.

MERMAID THREE. What about?

GRANDMER. It depends.

LITTLE MERMAID. But for instance.

GRANDMER. Over land.

LITTLE MERMAID. Land?

GRANDMER. One of them believes it belongs to them and another wants it for themselves.

MERMAID TWO. Why don't they share it?

GRANDMER. Or religion.

MERMAID ONE. What's that?

GRANDMER. Shsh, now. That's enough questions. Leave them.

The MERMAIDS *and* MEN *slowly stand except for the*
LITTLE MERMAID. *In slow motion, they take their human*
clothes from the wardrobe and dress.

LITTLE MERMAID. How strange and beautiful they are. What
does it all mean, Grandmer? What does it all mean?

GRANDMER. It means that life up above is full of pain and
suffering that we will never understand. It is better to forget
for there is nothing we can do to help them.

BLUE. But the more the mermaid heard about the world above,
the more she longed to see for herself. She vowed that she
would not be afraid. She would swim to the shore and follow
the sea up a river and into the heart of the city. She longed to
know how men live. To see into their hearts and understand
their secrets. At last the day came.

The youngest mermaid rose up, light as a bubble through
the water.

The LITTLE MERMAID *plunges her head into the water.*
She comes up soaking, as if she had just broken the surface
of the ocean. She is breathless.

LITTLE MERMAID. When I lifted my head above the water I
saw the beautiful, burning evening sky. I saw the hull of a
massive ship towering above me.

A ship is created. There is a royal party on board. Everyone
is dressed in elaborate, expensive clothes. They are singing
'Happy Birthday' to the sound of a military band.

BLUE. She heard the strange sound of human voices and swam
right up to a porthole and looked inside.

The KING *is holding a sword. The* PRINCE *is kneeling*
before him wearing his military uniform.

The LITTLE MERMAID *is transfixed.*

KING. It is with tremendous pride that today, on your
eighteenth birthday, I accept your oath of allegiance to our

great army. May you display courage and fearlessness in the face of our enemies and all who seek to destroy our country. May you lead our army to victory and defend all that is noble and righteous in the name of Almighty God.

The onstage audience repeats 'In the name of Almighty God'. We see the young PRINCE *rise. He grasps the handle of the sword, both afraid and excited. He feels its weight in his hand. He brandishes it in a mock-battle with the air. He laughs. He lashes out, anxious to prove his fearlessness to the crowd. The imaginary enemy becomes more and more real until finally he disembowels him, running him through again and again. The* PRINCE *looks at his own hand as if it belongs to someone else. The* LITTLE MERMAID *is transfixed. He is breathless.*

BLUE. At that moment a strange thing happened. The Prince looked through the porthole and into the eyes of the mermaid.

LITTLE MERMAID. I saw in his gaze a shifting sea of questions. I saw longing and fear and tenderness. I saw astonishing beauty, like moonlight on water, and I saw the depths of his loneliness.

BLUE. The mermaid felt as if she were drowning. Her heart began to pound. A cry rose in her throat.

She staggers, creating a great wave that sends the ship reeling. She sings. A storm begins. It is a physical manifestation of the LITTLE MERMAID*'s overwhelming excitement and confusion. The sea begins to pound the ship just as the* LITTLE MERMAID*'s heart pounds her chest.*

The royal party are flung across the deck as the ship reels in the water. The furniture slides back and forth across the deck and is swept overboard. Finally, a great wave overturns the vessel.

The royal party are swept into the water. In slow motion they struggle to remove their clothes. As the clothes come off the actors become the turbulent water around the LITTLE MERMAID *and* PRINCE.

The PRINCE, *deep in the water, struggles for his life, trying to remove his shoes and clothes in an effort to swim. The* LITTLE MERMAID *swims towards him. It is a terrifying journey through the violent waves.*

The LITTLE MERMAID *reaches the* PRINCE.

Slow-motion image of the PRINCE *buried under a deluge of waves created by the* MERMAIDS. *The water transforms his drowning movements into something spellbinding and beautiful.*

LITTLE MERMAID. Now, he will come down and live at the bottom of the ocean.

Slow-motion sequence. The LITTLE MERMAID *and the waves repeatedly smother the* PRINCE'S *mouth and drag him down into the ocean. His body grows limp and exhausted. He is at the point of losing consciousness.*

But then she remembered that man cannot live beneath the water. He would die if she did not save him.

She lifts his head above the water. He begins to breathe. She supports him with her body. Holding his head above the waves she swims towards the shore.

She drags him out of the water and pushes his body using her head onto the sand. The PRINCE *is unconscious. She sings to him. She is entranced by his body. His living flesh. Mesmerised, she examines his hand, his arm, his face. She longs to see him wake but her strength is failing. She cannot live out of the water.*

BLUE *walks towards the sea carrying a towel. She takes off her hoodie, revealing the top of her swimsuit. She puts on a pair of goggles. She is about to take off her jogging bottoms when she sees the* PRINCE *lying on the sand.*

BLUE *walks towards the body washed up on the beach. She cannot see the* LITTLE MERMAID. *She kneels down beside the body. Her movements mirror the* LITTLE MERMAID *although she is invisible to her.*

The LITTLE MERMAID *is becoming weaker. She sings to the* PRINCE.

BLUE *leans over the* PRINCE. *She looks for signs of life. His chest heaves and he retches. Her hands shaking,* BLUE *takes her mobile phone from her pocket and dials.*

BLUE. Ambulance. There's someone on the beach. At The Point. A man. He's ill but he's still breathing. I was about to swim and then I saw him. Please, please, come quickly.

The sound of an ambulance siren getting louder and louder. A PARAMEDIC *arrives and the* PRINCE *is placed on a gurney.*

The LITTLE MERMAID *heaves herself along the sand trying to follow, but her strength fails and she slithers back into the water and swims away unseen.*

Down below, GRANDMER *and the three* SISTERS *are awaiting the* LITTLE MERMAID'*s return. They are frightened. She swims towards them.*

They try to comfort her but sense that she is changed.

MERMAID ONE. What happened?

MERMAID TWO. Where have you been?

MERMAID ONE. We tried to find you but there was a terrible storm.

MERMAID TWO. You were gone so long we thought you were lost.

MERMAID THREE. What is it?

MERMAID TWO. Speak to us.

MERMAID ONE. Tell us. Please.

The PRINCE *is still on the gurney.* BLUE *stands beside him.*

BLUE. But she did not answer for she could not explain what had happened to her up above. She sat alone and stared up through the water towards the sky. For days on end she barely spoke, nor did she seem to hear. She swam back to the place where she had last seen the Prince but he was gone.

The LITTLE MERMAID *looks up through the water and sings with her* SISTERS *and the* CHOIR, *an aria-like song of longing. The sound rises to a crescendo.*

The PRINCE *stirs in his sleep. He is having a nightmare. Sitting up in his bed he cries out. His eyes are open but he does not see.*

BLUE *tries to comfort him. During the following dialogue, she sings the* LITTLE MERMAID*'s song. It calms him.*

Down below.

GRANDMER *goes to the* LITTLE MERMAID.

GRANDMER. What is it? Tell me.

LITTLE MERMAID (*fierce*). I felt his heart pound. I felt his weight upon my breast. His eyes were like moonlight on water. His skin smooth as untouched sand. If I never see him again I... I cannot live.

GRANDMER. Shshsh, child. You must not say such things.

LITTLE MERMAID. It's true.

GRANDMER. You must forget him.

LITTLE MERMAID. I can't.

GRANDMER. Listen to me. You must. No good can come of this.

LITTLE MERMAID. Forget him!

GRANDMER. Put him out of your mind.

LITTLE MERMAID. That's impossible.

GRANDMER. Never speak of this again. Not a word to your sisters or to anyone.

LITTLE MERMAID. Why –

GRANDMER. You belong here. You're safe here.

LITTLE MERMAID. I don't want to be safe. I want to live, and love, to *feel*.

GRANDMER. Enough. Believe me. It's for the best.

GRANDMER *leaves her.*

BLUE *sits beside the* PRINCE*'s bed in the hospital. The* PRINCE *stands and an* ORDERLY *brings him his military uniform. He stares at it as if trying to remember what it is.*

BLUE. And so the mermaid did not speak of him again but she thought of nothing else. At night she swam back to the place where she last saw the Prince, but it was deserted.

The PRINCE *slowly puts on his jacket and leaves.*

BLUE *walks towards the* LITTLE MERMAID.

She saw houses on the shore with lights glowing in the windows and she pulled herself up so that she could see inside. It was there that she saw the strangest sight.

The LITTLE MERMAID *peers inside. There is a news report on television. The sound of gunfire.*

A woman stared at a box, and in the box there were people, miniature people and the people in the box were speaking.

As the LITTLE MERMAID *describes the image, we see* BLUE*'s* MOTHER, *her face lit by a television screen. The sound of a news report from the war.*

Meanwhile BLUE*'s* FATHER *has entered the room. He has been drinking and stands for a moment steadying himself.*

MOTHER. Couldn't sleep. Been waiting up.

FATHER. No need.

MOTHER. Just one drink you said.

FATHER. Don't start.

MOTHER. Rent's overdue. She needs a new wetsuit. Old one's too small. And you promised her that surfboard from the catalogue for her birthday next week. Sixteen. We should make it special.

FATHER. I know how old she is.

MOTHER. And she wants the coach fare to go to the march next weekend.

FATHER. The march?

MOTHER. Stop the war. There's a big demonstration. They're saying there's going to be thousands. People from all over.

FATHER. You're going to let her go?

MOTHER. You try stopping her. She's set her heart on it. She's been making a banner in her bedroom out of an old sheet.

(*Tender.*) Her first rally. You remember when *we* used / to…

FATHER. I'm tired, going to bed.

MOTHER. You going down to the boats tomorrow? See if there's any work?

FATHER. Maybe.

BLUE *enters the room and sits beside her* MOTHER*'s chair and watches the television.*

MOTHER. She's been at the hospital again.

FATHER. They know who he is?

MOTHER. Totally confused, poor lad. Still out of it. Doesn't know his own name. Probably one of them homeless.

BLUE *turns up the volume on the television to hear a news report. Her* MOTHER *and* FATHER *leave.* BLUE *and the* LITTLE MERMAID *watch the following report.*

TV news. The sound of helicopters and waves.

NEWS REPORTER. Returning to our main story you can see that night is falling on the Atlantic. The search continues for the Prince who is still missing at sea over a hundred miles from land. It is forty-eight hours now since the vessel capsized during a celebration of the Prince's eighteenth birthday. A freak storm that defied weather forecasts swept the royal family overboard. The King and Queen were airlifted from the water and are currently recovering in hospital. Helicopters have been searching the icy water although it is thought to be impossible that the Prince could have survived the sub-zero temperatures. It seems there is no longer any hope of finding him alive. Thousands are filling the streets outside the Palace as they await news.

The sound of Big Ben striking the hour. MOTHER *turns off the television and fades into darkness as* BLUE *speaks.*

BLUE. For days and nights the search went on and the nation mourned. The Prince could not have survived the freezing waters a hundred miles from land.

The King and Queen had lost their only child.

Until one Sunday afternoon, there was a phone call.

During the above, the PALACE STAFF *set up chairs and serve the* QUEEN *a cup of tea from a tea set on a silver tray. The* KING *is hidden behind a newspaper.*

The QUEEN's PRIVATE SECRETARY *hurries into the room, agitated.*

PRIVATE SECRETARY. Excuse me, Your Highness, forgive me but I have some news that… cannot wait. It seems… it seems that… the Prince… unlikely as it sounds they believe that he… that he… has been found…

QUEEN. Dear God.

PRIVATE SECRETARY.…alive, Your Highness.

QUEEN. But how is that possible?

KING. It must be a hoax…

The QUEEN *sees her son walking towards her, his hair unkempt, his clothes dishevelled. She drops her tea cup and saucer. It clatters to the ground. She puts her hand to her mouth. The* PRINCE *looks around him and then at his mother as if struggling to remember who she is. The* QUEEN *stands but her legs buckle under her. She grips the edge of the table.*

QUEEN. Is it you? Is it really you?

PRINCE. I don't know.

Lights change. Camera flashes.

BLUE *is surrounded by a trio of* PHOTOGRAPHERS *and* JOURNALISTS *jostling for her attention, speaking over one another. The* PRINCE *remains on stage invisible to them.*

PHOTOGRAPHERS/JOURNALISTS. Blue, how did you feel after you saved the Prince?

What do you make of his survival?

People are calling this a miracle, would you agree?

You say you were going for a swim?

When did you realise it was His Royal Highness?

BLUE (*haltingly*). I didn't. He wasn't –

PHOTOGRAPHERS/JOURNALISTS. If you give me exclusive rights to the story I will make it well worth your while –

We can offer you a five-figure sum –

You and your family will be given –

Your dad's out of work, isn't he? Will fifty grand help?

BLUE (*pushes past*). No. I don't want – Leave me alone.

Lights change. The PRINCE *is staring into the river.*

The King and Queen wept with joy to see their beloved child. But the Prince was changed. Though they dared not say so he felt like a stranger. He would often walk alone in the Palace gardens at night. He would stand at the river's edge and look down into the black water as if he were searching for something.

One evening the mermaid waited until the others were asleep and then swam towards the shore.

The LITTLE MERMAID *plunges her head and hair into water.*

Late that night she swam up the river and deep into the heart of the dark city. Many times she had to dive down beneath the surface to avoid the rubbish that floated above. She saw strange sights. Buildings so high she feared they would topple into the water. She saw factories that spewed smoke into the air. She saw men whose bodies were blackened by dirt.

As the things the LITTLE MERMAID *sees are described, they come to life. It's a Friday night in the city.*

She heard the strange sounds made by lovers entwined under bridges. She saw drunkards laughing and fighting and children who shouted and threw stones.

CHILD ONE. What is that?

CHILD TWO. Oh my days –

CHILD THREE. What you chattin' about. I can't see nothing.

CHILD ONE. There's a girl in the water –

CHILD TWO. No, it's a fish –

CHILD ONE. It's a girl. Give me a stone.

The CHILDREN *throw a stone at the* LITTLE MERMAID. *She ducks out of sight.*

BLUE. She saw how people threw things they didn't want into the water.

The LITTLE MERMAID *swims tossing a plastic bag. She has never seen one before.*

As she swam into the heart of the city the sun rose over the turrets of a vast building.

LITTLE MERMAID. She heard the great clock strike the hour and remembered what Grandmer had told her about 'time' and how every moment it was passing.

BLUE. As she looked around her she saw that the city had changed. She saw the perfect green grass, the marble statues and fountains of the Palace gardens. Long-necked birds floated on the water, their feathers as white as the blossom on the trees.

The sound of birdsong. The LITTLE MERMAID *watches the* PRINCE *from beneath him in the water. He carries a book of philosophy which he is reading, trying to fathom.* BLUE *writes his words into the story.*

I think therefore I am.

PRINCE. 'I think therefore I am'… 'I think therefore I am'…

A SECURITY GUARD *approaches, talking into a mobile phone, informing the Palace that the* PRINCE *has been found.*

SECURITY GUARD. Excuse me, Your Highness, your regiment is awaiting inspection.

PRINCE.…or would it not be truer to say that it is 'thinking', the ceaseless chatter, the jabbering voices, the torrent of thoughts clamouring for attention. Is it not this very condition, that is unique to human beings, that distinguishes us from animals. Is it not this, this capacity for thought, the knowledge that we are alone in this world, that we are born and will so soon die. Is it not this very thinking that means I '*am*' not. That I cannot '*be*'. That I am trapped in my own head, looking on, peering at the world as if through the wrong end of a telescope.

SECURITY GUARD. The entire Royal Battalion has been standing to attention for the last half hour, Your Highness…

PRINCE. There is a tune. I cannot get it out of my head.

He begins to sing the LITTLE MERMAID'*s song. The* SECURITY GUARD *listens.*

SECURITY GUARD. Your father has requested that you return immediately / to the Palace.

PRINCE. Do you recognise it?

SECURITY GUARD. Excuse me?

PRINCE. Have you heard it before?

SECURITY GUARD. I… I… Couldn't say for certain. There being such a great many tunes and, I myself being less than musical –

PRINCE. It is strange but sometimes when I stand on this spot I hear it in the sound of the river.

SECURITY GUARD. Yes, sir.

PRINCE. Or perhaps it is on the wind.

The LITTLE MERMAID *sings. Only the* PRINCE *can hear it.*

Listen… There…

SECURITY GUARD. Your Highness, the King has requested that you return immediately to the Palace. He asked me to remind you respectfully, sir, of your recent escape. It is considered something of a miracle, your survival and return, the Palace is naturally anxious –

He can see that the PRINCE *is not listening.*

PRINCE. Did you ever hear such a sound?

SECURITY GUARD. I shall tell –

PRINCE. Shshshsh.

SECURITY GUARD. I shall tell the King that you –

PRINCE (*lowering his voice*). Does it not seem strange to you that I am attended night and day by people whose lives are devoted to my well-being. I am given every attention, my slightest utterance accorded significance, my opinion sought and my words repeated, as if this life of privilege did not render one utterly ill-equipped to know, to understand anything at all. (*Whispers.*) I know this and yet I dare not give up this charade, this… performance.

SECURITY GUARD. Your Majesty is still recovering –

PRINCE. They want me to marry. They think a wife will bring me to my senses. They have introduced me to every eligible young woman in the land. They think that a Royal Wedding will lift the spirits of the nation. Give them something to celebrate. A real-life fairy story to distract them.

But I can't, you see, because of the song.

SECURITY GUARD. The song?

PRINCE. I have to find out who sang it.

SECURITY GUARD. If you'll excuse me, Your Highness, I…

PRINCE. Do you believe that we have a soul? That it lives on when we die?

The SECURITY GUARD*'s mobile phone rings. He hurries away, talking into it.*

SECURITY GUARD. He's not going anywhere.

BLUE. Night after night the mermaid stared up at the Prince from the darkness of the river. Sometimes when the air was hot and the Palace slept he would walk into the water.

The PRINCE *wades out into the water. The* LITTLE MERMAID *is once again mesmerised. The sound of the* MERMAIDS *swells.*

She swims as close as she dares, almost touching his skin. He is totally unaware of her presence.

The PRINCE *leaves.* GRANDMER *comes to the* LITTLE MERMAID.

LITTLE MERMAID. Do you never wonder what it would be like to live above the water?

GRANDMER. You mustn't think of such things. We live far happier down here than they do up above. Men are always fighting and shouting and trying to prove how clever and important they are.

LITTLE MERMAID. Why?

GRANDMER. Because they're afraid.

LITTLE MERMAID. What of?

GRANDMER. That someone will find out that they're afraid.

LITTLE MERMAID. I don't understand.

GRANDMER. Of all the animals on earth, man alone knows that
he must die. And so he longs to cheat death, to forget his
mortality. He builds and he buys and he conquers. He tries to
believe, to have faith. He snatches at pleasure. Gorges himself
on whatever scraps he can find. But all the time he knows that
his hour is coming. That soon he will be foam on the ocean.

LITTLE MERMAID (*passionate*). But what about 'love'?

GRANDMER. Enough.

LITTLE MERMAID. What about the soul? Do I have a soul?

GRANDMER. That's enough questions.

LITTLE MERMAID. Does every human have a one?

Please tell me. If you don't I'll go back and find out for
myself.

Beat.

GRANDMER. They have one but I doubt they will ever find it.

LITTLE MERMAID. How is that possible?

GRANDMER. Man's suffering, if it doesn't destroy him or
send him mad, it can teach him things.

If he dares to open his heart, if he is able to abandon his fear,
his pride, then he can know the pain and joy of others, feel it
as if it were his own. That is 'love' and in this is man's
salvation, the soul that lives on for ever.

LITTLE MERMAID. Oh, Grandmer. That is what I long for. To
see into his soul, to know his pain and joy, to hear his secrets
and for him to know mine.

GRANDMER. You must put these thoughts out of your mind.

LITTLE MERMAID. The song I sang on the night of the storm,
the night I rescued him, he says he cannot marry until he has
found out who sang it. I have to go to him.

GRANDMER. But that will never be. The love that you long
for, it will never happen. You cannot live on the land and he
will drown in the ocean.

The KING *stands in front of a mirror with a* MEMBER OF
THE PALACE STAFF *doing up his cufflinks. He speaks as if
to the* QUEEN, *offstage.*

KING. I understand, it is only natural that you should be
protective, after everything… But you do him no favours by
keeping him locked away, swaddled up in the Palace. It's
little wonder he is so preoccupied with nothing to do all day
but think. Action. Discipline, that's what he needs. A man
must test himself, prove his worth, his mettle. There is
nothing like a war to bring a boy to his senses.

QUEEN. You're right of course. I know he must return to the
regiment.

KING. You'll see. It will be for the best.

QUEEN. And yet I fear for him. If only we could find him a
wife. Someone, something to bring him home.

As she speaks, the PRINCE *crosses the stage in combat gear.
He stops in front of his father and mother and waves in slow
motion to the crowds. He leaves.*

The QUEEN *straightens the* KING*'s tie and then stands back
and nods approval. They leave.*

BLUE. The next time the mermaid swam up above, the air was
cold.

The LITTLE MERMAID *plunges her head into the water.
She comes up shivering. Snow falling into water.*

She had never seen the winter before, for down below there
were no seasons. She saw the skeletons of the trees and the
snow fall into the black water and the water turn to ice.

LITTLE MERMAID. The Prince no longer came down to the
river, although I sang and waited and sang again. I feared
that I would never see him again. One day I heard people

talking about the war far away where the Prince was fighting. There was a newspaper thrown into the river with his face upon it. He was holding a gun.

The LITTLE MERMAID *looks at a piece of crumpled newspaper with a photo of the* PRINCE *in a war zone.*

The PRINCE *comes out from under the platform with a gun. He climbs up onto the platform firing his gun as if trying to protect something behind him. We hear the sound of a crying child. He moves backwards across the stage, firing as he goes. He disappears.*

BLUE. She realised that she would always be invisible to the world of men. That she would never know what it is to love and be loved. Soon she became sick with longing and could not eat or sleep. Her hair fell out in handfuls and her body grew thin. She knew that there was only one person who could help her. And so, one night, too afraid to tell her sisters, she swam off towards the forbidden wreck. Deep inside lived the Sea Witch, once a mermaid who sacrificed all to try and win the love of a mortal.

The SEA WITCH *is played by four women as one mass of seething limbs and heads. Her movements are based on sea predators so the scene has a tension, as if the* LITTLE MERMAID *might be eaten alive. She wears an assortment of staggeringly high heels on her eight feet. She wears basques and corsets and pieces of rubber-and-plastic S&M underwear. She has strange surgical gloves and she looks as if she has had extensive plastic surgery, her face pulled tight. She is bald but for a few wispy strands of hair.*

The SEA WITCH *is half-fish, half-human and can scarcely see and so comes strangely close to the* LITTLE MERMAID.

Divide up the SEA WITCH*'s lines between the four actors. Some lines may be echoed or repeated by the others.*

SEA WITCH. At last, I thought you would never come.

LITTLE MERMAID. How did you know…

SEA WITCH. You are not the first nor will you be the last.

LITTLE MERMAID. What do you / mean?

SEA WITCH. I can see it in your eyes, smell it, the longing. I remember. I remember. (*Stops herself.*) Don't worry, my dear, you have come to the right person, you will not be disappointed. You shall have your heart's desire. All that you long for shall be yours.

LITTLE MERMAID. I want to live above the water.

SEA WITCH. I know.

LITTLE MERMAID. To walk, to breathe –

SEA WITCH. Of course.

LITTLE MERMAID. To lose my fish tail and live as if I were born up above.

SEA WITCH. All this and more I can give you.

LITTLE MERMAID. How?

The SEA WITCH *holds out a bottle.*

SEA WITCH. Drink this and you will have the woman's body that you long for. Tomorrow morning at sunrise your tail will divide and become two perfect legs.

LITTLE MERMAID. Oh, thank you. Thank you…

She tries to take the bottle but the SEA WITCH *snatches it.*

SEA WITCH. It will cost you.

LITTLE MERMAID. Just tell me what you want.

SEA WITCH. It is no small payment.

LITTLE MERMAID. Ask and it is yours.

SEA WITCH. I have heard you sing. You have the most beautiful voice in the ocean. I expect you have thought of using that voice to charm your Prince, but that will never be. When you open your mouth to speak no sound will come out, for that voice you will have given to me.

LITTLE MERMAID. My voice!

SEA WITCH. Unless you win the heart of a mortal you will never utter another sound.

LITTLE MERMAID. But how will I make him love me if I cannot speak? How will I tell him who I am or where I have come from?

SEA WITCH. Who you are? (*Howls with laughter.*) You think he wants to know who you are? To hear your childish thoughts. Do you think a prince would be interested in your foolish prattle. You who have only ever lived at the bottom of the ocean and know nothing of the world. My dear, that tongue of yours will be a liability. Far better without it. You won't be tempted to spoil your beauty.

LITTLE MERMAID. I don't understand.

SEA WITCH (*reaching towards the* LITTLE MERMAID *as if mesmerised by her perfect skin*). Up above there is one thing that is more precious than life itself. One thing for which man will sacrifice all. You have never seen yourself in a mirror but when you do you will see that you possess the greatest prize of all. On earth to be beautiful is everything. Use your perfect body, your lustrous hair, your radiant smile, your shining eyes. (*She is so close she is almost touching the* LITTLE MERMAID.) Speak with them.

LITTLE MERMAID. But I want to hear his secrets. To tell him mine. To know him as I know myself –

SEA WITCH. I was once like you. Full of foolish dreams and longings. I too imagined that I could have everything.

LITTLE MERMAID (*disturbed, staring at the* SEA WITCH). What happened? What happened to you?

SEA WITCH (*hissing, furious*). How dare you. Get out of my sight. Get away from me.

She grabs the potion. She goes to pour it on the ground.

The LITTLE MERMAID *snatches the vial from her.*

LITTLE MERMAID. NO! Do it now quickly. I shall not flinch.

The SEA WITCH *looks at the* LITTLE MERMAID *and suddenly clasps her hair in her hands. She takes out a knife. She is about to chop out the* LITTLE MERMAID*'s tongue when the* LITTLE MERMAID *recoils.*

SEA WITCH. What is it now?

LITTLE MERMAID. I…

She cannot go on.

SEA WITCH. I am losing my patience.

LITTLE MERMAID. I…

SEA WITCH. What?

LITTLE MERMAID. Unless I win the heart of a mortal I will never sing again?

SEA WITCH. Never.

LITTLE MERMAID. Nor laugh. Nor cry. Nor utter any sound.

SEA WITCH. That is correct.

LITTLE MERMAID. It's… terrible.

SEA WITCH. Nonsense. It will help you bear the agony of love without crying out loud.

LITTLE MERMAID. But, if I have no voice, what will I have left? Who will I become?

SEA WITCH (*angry*). Enough. You are wasting my time –

LITTLE MERMAID (*suddenly*). Let it happen.

The SEA WITCH *cuts out her tongue. Blood gushes from her mouth and runs down her neck. The* SEA WITCH *puts the* LITTLE MERMAID*'s tongue into a jar and screws on the lid.*

Another tentacle gives the LITTLE MERMAID *the potion.*

SEA WITCH. Remember to smile. If you do not smile he will never love you and all will be lost.

I thank you for your tongue. It will give me much pleasure.

She opens the lid and we hear the LITTLE MERMAID*'s voice sing from the jar. The sound of the* LITTLE MERMAID*'s singing, amplified a thousand times, comes from every direction. The* SEA WITCHES *pass the jar between them in a frenzy of orgasmic pleasure. She snaps the lid back on and barks.*

Away with you. Out of my sight.

The LITTLE MERMAID *swims away and onto the banks of the river. She drinks the potion as the first light of morning touches the sky. She falls to the ground.*

Interval.

ACT TWO

The LITTLE MERMAID *lying on the bank of the river that flows through the Palace gardens. Sound of birdsong and tinkling water.*

She awakes and looks out at the gardens. She sees the perfect grass and the blossom trees then, suddenly, sees her own two legs. She starts with surprise. She lifts one leg with her hand and then the other. It's as if they do not belong to her.

The PRINCE *walks towards her.*

PRINCE. Who are you?

> *The* LITTLE MERMAID *scuttles backwards along the ground.*

> How did you get into the Palace gardens? Where did you come from?

> BLUE *is now wearing Dr. Martens and a tie-dye top.*

BLUE. Although the Prince could remember nothing of the night of the storm, something stirred deep inside him. Waves crashed over his heart. The Prince looked into her sea-green eyes and felt as if he were drowning.

PRINCE (*to the* LITTLE MERMAID). Who are you?

> *The* LITTLE MERMAID *tries to raise herself up but she cannot stand.*

> Come, let me help you.

> *The* LITTLE MERMAID *is helped to her feet. Like a foal trying to stand for the first time, she sways and staggers and finally falls. The* PRINCE *lifts her up in his arms and carries her.*

He enters the Palace dining room where the QUEEN *is
signing royal invitations and the* KING *is reading the
newspaper. A* BUTLER *in attendance.*

QUEEN. Since returning from the war he has taken to
wandering the grounds all hours of the night and day.
Yesterday he was found by one of the gardeners waist-deep
in the river tearing petals off a crimson rose. One can hardly
forbid him from walking in his own garden but...

The PRINCE *stands holding the dripping* LITTLE
MERMAID *in his arms. She is fascinated by the strange
world of the Palace and leans back in his arms looking at the
room upside down.*

The KING *looks up from behind his newspaper at the*
LITTLE MERMAID.

PRINCE. Mother. Father.

KING. Good God. What on earth?

PRINCE. I would like to introduce you.

The PRINCE *places the* LITTLE MERMAID *on a chair. She
does not know how to sit on a chair and still moves like a
mermaid with her legs like a tail.*

QUEEN. Thank the Lord. (*Silencing the* KING.) At last. We
thought it would never happen. (*To the* LITTLE
MERMAID.) It is a great pleasure to meet you. Welcome to
the Palace.

KING. But –

QUEEN (*to the* PRINCE). Congratulations, my dear.

KING. But who is she? –

QUEEN. What marvellous news.

KING. News? Forgive me, dear girl, but who are you?

The LITTLE MERMAID *tries to speak but no sound comes
from her mouth. She tries again. She turns back to the*
PRINCE.

PRINCE (*realising*). You can't speak.

The QUEEN *stands and speaks to the* LITTLE MERMAID.

QUEEN. No matter. Tonight we shall have a banquet in honour
of your engagement. You will be bathed and dressed by my
very own ladies-in-waiting. There is nothing to be afraid of.
With a little help you will do very well.

The LADIES-IN-WAITING *arrive with their beauty
equipment to loud classical music. The* LITTLE MERMAID
*is transformed into a Kate Middleton-esque mannequin. Her
body hair is removed with wax strips, razors and tweezers.
She makes as if to cry out in pain but no sound comes from
her mouth. Lipstick is applied to her lips. She is thrust into
tightly fitting clothes, a dress with a cinched-in waist and
perilously high heels. Her hair is twisted into a clasp and a
tiara placed on her head as hairspray is squirted at her hair.*

When she tries to walk she staggers. The LADIES-IN-
WAITING *support her and then give her a demonstration of
how to walk in heels and she copies, gradually taking on
their physicality.*

The LITTLE MERMAID *looks in the mirror. The* LADIES-
IN-WAITING *leave. She moves and realises that the person
in the mirror moves too. She reaches out towards herself as if
confused. She touches the glass and then looks behind it. She
looks again at herself and then touches her own face, her
hair, her dress. She turns away and then looks behind her to
see if the person in the mirror is still there.*

The QUEEN *puts a ring on her finger. She speaks quietly
into the* LITTLE MERMAID*'s ear.*

Look at yourself. *That* is who you are now.

BLUE. The mermaid felt a strange chill growing inside her. But
that night she stood at the Prince's side. Eyes followed her
wherever she went and voices whispered envious approval.
Everyone who saw her agreed that she was the most
exquisite creature that they had ever seen.

ROYAL GUESTS *in lavish hats and fascinators mingle and greet the* LITTLE MERMAID. *The* PRINCE *leads the* LITTLE MERMAID *to the middle of the dance floor. They dance a waltz.*

Everyone waltzes whilst watching the PRINCE *and the* LITTLE MERMAID. *They peel away leaving the* PRINCE *and* LITTLE MERMAID *dancing alone.*

Could it be? Could it be that he had fallen in love? That she had won his heart, and would sing again? Could it be?

Lights change. The PRINCE *and* LITTLE MERMAID *are surrounded by paparazzi. Microphones are thrust forward and voices clamour for attention. Each line goes to a different* JOURNALIST.

JOURNALISTS. Where did you propose?

When's the big day?

Who's going to design the dress?

Tell us about the engagement ring. We've heard it's Bulgari –

Or Tiffany's?

When's the wedding day?

Wearing an exquisite jewelled tiara and an elegant aquamarine evening dress, our guess would be Chanel or maybe Temperley.

Could this be a clue as to who will design the wedding dress?

Tell us. How did he pop the question? Did the Prince get down on one knee?

A microphone is thrust at the LITTLE MERMAID. *The* LITTLE MERMAID *is blinded by camera flashes. She stares out at the sea of faces. She opens her mouth but no sound comes out.*

PRINCE. That's enough questions for today, thank you.

As before, each line goes to a different JOURNALIST. *The lines can overlap a little.*

JOURNALISTS. Your Highness, when will you be going back to the war?

Is it true you abandoned your regiment because you were failing to cope under the pressure?

Do you feel you're letting our troops down by deserting them at this crucial stage in the campaign?

Ten soldiers were killed yesterday. What message do you have for their families?

How do you feel about your friends and comrades under constant attack from the enemy?

Is it true you're suffering from post-traumatic stress?

Another explosion of camera flashes trigger a violent dream.

The PRINCE *is in the middle of a war. The camera flashes turn into explosions and gunfire. He is facing a barrage of bullets. Everyone runs for cover. People are shot down, falling to the ground and being dragged away. The* PRINCE *fires rounds of bullets from a machine gun. The* LITTLE MERMAID *is shot. He lifts her trying to bring her back to life. The sounds of explosions turn in to the sound of a storm.*

The PRINCE *dreams that he is drowning. It is a re-enactment of the original sequence in which the* LITTLE MERMAID *saved him from the storm. The drowning has taken on a new quality as the violence of the war permeates the struggle. He awakes suddenly sweating and afraid.*

BLUE. I dreamt… I have terrible dreams…

PRINCE. I dreamt… I have terrible dreams. I'm back in the icy water… (*Explains.*) That night I nearly drowned. I have no memory of how I survived. I remember only a beautiful song that filled my head and haunts me still.

The LITTLE MERMAID *tries to sing.*

BLUE. The song rose up in her throat like a great wave but no sound came. How she longed to tell the Prince that she had been his saviour. How she ached to sing again.

PRINCE. What is it? Tell me? Speak to me.

He holds her face. She looks up at the sky to fight back her tears.

As the PRINCE *speaks we hear distant sounds of war.*

BLUE (*writing the* PRINCE'*s words*). You know that I am soon to return to the war.

PRINCE. You know that I am soon to return to the war. Join the battalion. Last night, I was watching… on the news. There had been a suicide bomb and people were protesting in the square. It was just as I remembered, the street vendors and the children playing football with a tin can and, and then suddenly, there were tanks, our tanks, driven by our soldiers, careering through the crowds, as if the people were skittles. There was a woman screaming. She was holding the body of a child, that's what it said, but you couldn't tell. You couldn't tell what it was there was so much blood… And afterwards, rows of bodies, lying under sheets, faceless, nameless. We, here, we live under the illusion that our lives are… of significance. We cannot allow ourselves to imagine that these people, these strangers, feel things just as we do. We have to believe that their helplessness is a sign of their inferiority, their failure. That they somehow deserve their fate, just as we deserve ours. Perhaps this illusion is necessary. Without it we are faced with the knowledge of our own staggering insignificance. We are those people ploughed down by the tank. We are the mother holding her dying child, helpless in the face of its suffering. We are the children who asked us for sweets one morning and were hung from a tree when we returned that night, punished for talking to soldiers.

BLUE. The mermaid remembered what Grandmer had told her about the land above. How it was full of pain and suffering but there was nothing they could do to help them.

PRINCE. I'm sorry. I'm so sorry. I shouldn't frighten you.

Let's play a game. Let's pretend, let's pretend that we're happy.

Lights change.

BLUE. The Prince would wonder where she had come from. But she could not tell him and he could only guess.

The LITTLE MERMAID *tries to mime being a mermaid.*

PRINCE. You are… (*Playfully.*) a Russian spy who dropped into the ocean and swam to shore?

She mimes again.

A princess who was kidnapped and escaped on a boat.

The LITTLE MERMAID *shakes her head.*

…An orphan who was abandoned at sea?

She mimes diving through the waves.

A mermaid?

There is a sudden charge between them.

There was a story my nanny used to tell me over and over until I knew it by heart. It had an unhappy ending and I used always to wish it might end differently.

He studies her. She suddenly, impulsively kisses him on the lips. She pulls back and looks at the PRINCE *to gauge his reaction. She kisses him again and he slowly begins to respond, yielding to the moment. There is a growing hunger to their embrace until the* PRINCE *suddenly pulls away and turns his back on the* LITTLE MERMAID. *He can hear the sounds of battle.*

The war, it keeps coming back. It's like I'm still there. I can't. I'm sorry.

Lights change.

The LADIES-IN-WAITING *adjust the* LITTLE
MERMAID*'s hair and make-up. The* QUEEN *fastens a
diamond necklace around her neck. The* KING *and* QUEEN
wave to the crowds. The LITTLE MERMAID *joins the*
PRINCE *at the centre of the photograph. She waves and
smiles. We hear the news recordings, each sentence read by
a different* NEWS REPORTER. *They overlap.*

NEWS REPORTERS. Three months since their engagement
and still no date is set for / the wedding.

She has been seen alone *again* this week prompting
speculation / about the Prince's absence.

As the Princess gets thinner there are rumours that she
isn't eating.

The body language between the royal couple suggests a
cooling / between them.

So far the Princess has failed to find her role and seems to be
struggling / to cope with the demands of...

Wearing too much make-up that scarcely disguises the dark
rings / under her eyes.

The Princess was seen without make-up looking distinctly /
pale.

Seen wearing an exquisite diamond necklace from the
Queen's own collection, the Princess is looking tired and
drawn.

The PRINCE *dutifully puts his arm around the* LITTLE
MERMAID. *She goes to kiss him but he pulls away.*

BLUE. The Prince told her no more of his fears and longings.
He dared not burden her with his thoughts.

As the NEWS REPORTERS' *words repeat in a babble in her
head, the* LITTLE MERMAID *goes to the mirror and looks
at herself, her lipstick is smudged and her face pale. She
tries to adjust her clothes and hair. She starts to pull at her
face, becoming increasingly violent as if she were trying to*

*rub herself out. She sticks her fingers down her throat and
vomits. The* PRINCE *walks up to her and she tries to clean
her mouth with her hand. There is an awkward moment
before he moves on.*

The PRINCE *and* LITTLE MERMAID *go to sit at an
elegant table. The* WAITER *lifts the lid on a silver platter to
reveal a fish.*

That night the mermaid sat down for a royal banquet with a
heavy heart. Seared sea bass was served on a bed of scallops.
She turned as pale as the napkin.

The LITTLE MERMAID *drops the platter with a mighty
clatter. She falls to her knees and tries to clear the mess. The
three* ATTENDANTS *all scurry about on the floor trying to
retrieve the cutlery and food. It is clear she has made a
terrible faux pas. She runs from the room in tears.*

Fish was never served again.

The PRINCE *follows her trying to think of something to say
to comfort her.*

PRINCE. My mother is impatient for us to marry. She thinks
that a wedding will lift the spirits of the nation, distract them
from the war.

BLUE. But he said no more. For days, the Prince was silent. It
was as if he scarcely saw her.

Lights change.

During the following speech, the LITTLE MERMAID *sits
on the riverbank and removes her high-heeled shoes. She
puts her aching feet into the water and then her hands and
hair. She stretches into the current as if remembering deep
in her body the weightlessness and freedom of her life as a
mermaid.*

At night the mermaid would go down to the river that ran
through the Palace gardens. How she longed to show the
Prince the beauty of the world beneath the water. To dance
with shoals of fish in the moonlight and sing to the stars in

the middle of the ocean. She longed to tell him of her sisters and the things that she had loved and lost. She remembered how it felt to have a tail, to be light and weightless and free, to know nothing of the suffering of the world.

The MERMAID SISTERS *appear but the* MERMAID *cannot see them.*

The mermaid began to dream at night of her sisters. That they were swimming together up towards the surface of the water. When she awoke she felt a terrible gnawing emptiness. She longed to sleep and dream again.

The SISTERS *put their heads out of the water just as the* MERMAID *turns away. They reach towards her.*

The PRINCE *enters and lies beside the water, stirring the currents with his hand. Beneath the water the* MERMAIDS *shift slowly in the current.*

The QUEEN *enters. She clears her throat.*

QUEEN. My dear. The time has come. We must name the day. I know you don't want to be rushed but the date must be decided before you return to the regiment. It will give the nation something to look forward to. A celebration. The August bank holiday is probably the best hope for decent weather although hardly reliable, but then we will have to prepare for rain as well as sunshine.

PRINCE (*distracted, staring into the river*). Not now.

QUEEN. But, my dear, this cannot go on. Months and still no talk of a wedding day. You must see that this is becoming an embarrassment.

PRINCE. Embarrassment?

QUEEN. The entire country is speculating as to why there is no announcement –

PRINCE. I said not now.

QUEEN. Why ever not? What is the matter?

BLUE. I dreamt I was a butterfly.

PRINCE. I dreamt I was a butterfly. Or am I a butterfly dreaming that I'm a man? What do you think, Mother?

QUEEN. I think you should be married, as soon as possible.

PRINCE. Butterflies you see, they only live for a few days, or sometimes weeks if they are not devoured by some other creature, but those few days, they are an eternity, having no knowledge of past or future, no knowledge even of its own astonishing beauty, it lives unaware of our gaze, unaware of anything but its own pulsing life, an ecstasy of now and now and now, so that even as they are about to be eaten alive the moment before their extinction is beautiful.

The QUEEN *is wringing her hands.*

QUEEN. I have no idea what you're talking about.

PRINCE. We live in fear.

QUEEN. Fear?

PRINCE. Of all the creatures on earth, mankind is the only one to realise that it is himself that he sees in the mirror. It is our curse, is it not, Mother. The desire to impress, to show only what is admirable, what is enviable in ourselves. Hide that of which we are ashamed.

QUEEN (*struggling*). I know, I realise that you are unhappy, but there's nothing... I can't...

PRINCE. This life that we lead, the pomp and ceremony, does it never strike you as absurd?

QUEEN. I shall tell the press office that a date will be decided before the / weekend.

PRINCE. The war, it was a relief in a way, to be in the middle of a battle, to forget everything else, to know that if you didn't kill them then they would kill you. To have something real to be afraid of.

Beat.

QUEEN. There is to be a twenty-one-gun salute followed by a firework display to mark your return to the regiment. You are required to do nothing more than stand beside her on the deck and applaud when it is over. I trust you will do as I ask and no more.

Sound of waves. Cannons. Fireworks. The KING, QUEEN, PRINCE *and the* LITTLE MERMAID *in formal dress stand on deck.*

PRINCE. Tomorrow night I will be far from here. Perhaps it will be better that way. I can see that I am a burden to all including myself. Neither foolish enough *not* to see the absurdity of my life, nor courageous enough to change it. Forgive me.

A song is heard on the breeze. The MERMAIDS *are singing.*

Remember once I told you that I heard a beautiful song that night I nearly drowned. It is strange, but sometimes, when I'm near the water, for a moment it comes back. I can hear it now.

The singing swells. They are both affected by the sound.

When I return I will marry you.

BLUE. At last the words she had longed to hear and yet, how could he love her, for everything that she once was had been lost. Who would she *be*, silent at his side? Nothing. Nobody. She would rather be foam on the ocean.

Lights change. The next day.

The PRINCE *shakes the* KING*'s hand and kisses the* QUEEN *goodbye. The* LITTLE MERMAID *walks forward towards the cheering crowds, shaking hands. The* LITTLE MERMAID *is wearing dark glasses and a wide-brimmed hat. Crowds cheer and wave. We hear the sound of news reports following the event live.*

NEWS REPORTERS. The royal couple are leaving the Palace on their way to the naval base before the Prince sets sail. You can hear the crowds outside the Palace. We can catch a glimpse of His Highness in full military dress with his fiancée beside him in a powder-blue coat.

We can just about see her there wearing dark glasses. Concerns that she has lost weight / have dominated recent reports...

The Prince's return to his regiment is seen by many as an attempt to rally support for an increasingly unpopular war that has become a thorn / in the side of the...

As the death toll mounts, the Prince is coming under criticism / for his absence from the public eye.

Questions over the Prince's ability to lead / his regiment...

His relationship with his fiancée seems to have done little to support the / Prince.

The couple are rarely seen together, fuelling rumours that there is a serious rift / in their relationship...

The public are starting to suspect that the Princess has an eating disorder / or is she just...

Stories of her bingeing and vomiting in secret are becoming difficult to ignore.

As the car travels along the coast towards the naval base, the crowds at the gates are about to be rewarded for their long wait.

Some have been here since yesterday, camping out to secure the best position to witness the arrival of His Royal Highness and his fiancée. There are others who have come here to protest against the war. We hope that this won't delay the Prince's departure. As you can see they are making their presence felt.

We hear crowds of PROTESTERS *carrying banners with slogans against the war. They jostle and shout as the* PRINCE'*s cavalcade grows close. We see* BLUE *shouting amidst the throng. She is waving a huge anti-war banner with silver thread and shells. A wonderful thing that she has made herself. She has grown into a beautiful young woman with a grace and style of her own. The banner ripples across the stage as she shouts and we hear the* PROTESTERS *roar around her.*

We hear the sound of the sea and BLUE *speaks.*

BLUE. Through the car window, the mermaid saw the shimmering ocean. She heard the sound of the waves like a calling. Her heart began to pound.

The LITTLE MERMAID *steps out of the car and towards the beach where* BLUE *is now sitting.*

The LITTLE MERMAID *sees the ocean and in slow motion tears off her hat and necklace and dark glasses. She starts to struggle out of her clothes as if they were a tourniquet, finally wriggling out of her dress and shoes so that she is once more a mermaid. Her* SISTERS *have appeared in the ocean.*

The LITTLE MERMAID *is at the edge of the ocean when she sees* BLUE *watching her. There is a sudden charge as they recognise one another and slowly reach out as if to touch their own reflection. They mirror one another.*

A sequence where the two meld and become one. The LITTLE MERMAID *starts to sing as never before, her voice rising in an aria of unearthly sound.*

The PRINCE *appears on the beach. He follows the trail of clothes towards* BLUE *and the* LITTLE MERMAID.

The LITTLE MERMAID *and* BLUE *are entwined. Throughout the following dialogue, the* LITTLE MERMAID *is singing on tape. The* PRINCE *sees the* LITTLE MERMAID *and* BLUE *as if they were one.*

PRINCE. The song you're singing. Where does it come from? Where did you learn it?

BLUE (*reading from her story*). You remember?

PRINCE. I heard it once, many years ago. It has filled my thoughts ever since but I never heard anyone sing it until now. Tell me, where did you hear it?

BLUE. The day I found you on the beach it was as if the sea was singing.

PRINCE. Found me?

BLUE. There had been a storm, at first I thought you had drowned. Your flesh was bruised and your eyes closed but then I saw that you were breathing. You were taken to hospital. You remembered nothing, not even your own name. You spoke in strange broken sentences. Cried out in your sleep. I sang you the song I heard that night of the storm. It seemed to comfort you. I told you the story of the mermaid that I was read as a child. I told you how in my dreams I used to dive down deep into the sea and swim with the mermaids and sing to the stars. The dream was so real that when I awoke I could think of nothing else. All day I longed to sleep and dream again.

BLUE *stands, taking the* PRINCE*'s hand and pulling him towards the sea. The* LITTLE MERMAID *slips into the ocean, joining her* SISTERS *in a dance of joy.*

(*To the* PRINCE.) Come. Come and swim in the ocean.

BLUE *steps into the sea and joins the* MERMAIDS. *The* MERMAIDS *and the* CHOIR *sing.*

The PRINCE *starts to take off his jacket and shoes.* BLUE *walks through the mermaid sea. She puts her head into the water and then suddenly lifts her head. Splashes cascade all around her. The* MERMAIDS *dance.*

The sound of the helicopters and sirens gets louder and louder. We hear the SECURITY GUARD *speaking into his phone. Just as the* PRINCE *is about to step into the ocean the* SECURITY GUARD *takes hold of his shoulder.*

The sound of television news reportage covering the event live. The helicopter is overhead.

Recorded news reports as security take the PRINCE *by the shoulder, pulling him away from the* MERMAIDS *and back onto the shore.*

RECORDED NEWS. There is a serious breach in security with the Prince and Princess no longer inside the vehicle. It seems that the Princess has disappeared without trace.

The Prince has joined a young woman, an activist from the demonstration, who is now swimming out into the sea.

Much to the astonishment of the crowds, the Prince is removing his shoes.

Efforts are being made to return the Prince to the vehicle and proceed towards the naval base.

No one seems to be sure how the Princess managed to evade the security services.

Questions will be asked about the efficacy of operations in the face of this extraordinary event.

The PRINCE *is escorted backwards away from the* MERMAIDS, *in slow motion, still struggling.*

BLUE *and the* LITTLE MERMAID *reach out towards the* PRINCE *but he is wrestled away.*

Lights change as the sounds recede.

The sound of the beach, the waves on the shingle and the gulls. BLUE *and the* LITTLE MERMAID *make their way back to the shore and then sit entwined.* BLUE *picks up her exercise book to complete the story.*

BLUE. Ever since I was a child I have loved more than anything to swim in the ocean. I once believed that I could hear mermaids singing in a shell I kept under my pillow, and that when I swam I had a tail.

BLUE'*s* MOTHER *stands behind her. She watches as* BLUE *closes the book.*

There is a swell of sound as the MERMAIDS *flick their tails with joy.*

An Interview with Polly Teale

Can you remember first hearing The Little Mermaid *story?*

As a child I was first bewitched by the tale of *The Little Mermaid*. I had it on a record and would play it and sit and sob on the settee, much to the bewilderment of my brothers. It wasn't until years later that I found myself wondering what it was about this dark coming-of-age story, about a mermaid who had her tongue cut out, that spoke to me so powerfully.

At the centre of the story is the experience of puberty and the self-consciousness that comes with it, a sort of loss of self.

The mermaids live beneath the ocean in a state of unselfconscious freedom until they come of age and swim up to the surface to see the world above. Leaving behind the (amniotic fluid of the) ocean, the mermaid is suddenly confronted by herself as a separate entity in a vast universe. From this moment there is no going back to safety. She has glimpsed the world in all its beauty and brutality and in that same instance fallen in love with a mortal Prince. She can no longer remember what it is to feel complete within herself. For the first time in her life she experiences desire and with it comes loneliness. She must live beneath the ocean, invisible to the world of men, or else sacrifice her tongue, her voice in order to walk and try to gain the Prince's love. She is warned that every step she takes she will feel like she is walking on knives.

It seems that even my ten-year-old self understood that there was something in this impossible choice that I could recognise. As a girl I sensed that, to leave behind childhood was to risk losing the freedom to exist on your own terms, to sacrifice your voice in order to try to please others, to gain their approval and love. The mermaid's sacrifice, her reliance on her physical beauty to win the Prince, expressed an uncomfortable reality. Whatever I might be inside it was what I looked like that determined my value.

Do you think that is particularly true today with so much advertising and imagery everywhere we look?

In an age of mass media, of Facebook, Instagram and Snapchat, we are constantly looking at our own reflections and at idealised images of others. We spend vast amounts of money on beauty products. Dieting is an obsession and use of plastic surgery has quadrupled in ten years. Fifty thousand women had invasive procedures in Britain last year. Removing body hair has become the norm. It feels like this is a story with increasing relevance. It's not surprising that we are seeing an epidemic of self-harm amongst teenage girls. As women obsess about calories and totter around in six-inch heels to make themselves appear thinner, the mermaid's story speaks of the extreme lengths that women will go to alter themselves to win approval and of the crippling self-consciousness that can characterise modern life.

That's not to say that we shouldn't enjoy styling and decorating ourselves. That is an innate human instinct that we see in all humans, even in tribes in remote places who have no access to mirrors. It can be a source of pleasure and creativity if it is not based in a sense of lack, of inadequacy.

Do the mermaids know what they look like?

No they don't. It is strange to think that it is only relatively recently that ordinary people have had access to mirrors. I often wonder how it would alter our sense of self if we had no idea how we appeared to others. I decided that in the world beneath the ocean there were no mirrors, that the mermaids would not know what they looked like. They would be unselfconsciously curious, like very young children or animals, living inside their bodies looking out at the world, not watching themselves with a critical gaze. It is not until they witness the world above that they understand themselves to be separate beings who are visible to others. With this understanding comes self-consciousness and the knowledge of our essential aloneness, of death, of anxiety, of need and desire. In my version of the story the mermaids are immortal. Beneath the ocean there is no time.

Would you say that in the play we are looking at our human world through the eyes of the mermaids?

Yes. I wanted to see our world through their eyes in all its strangeness. To see the arbitrary hierarchies that exist, how simply by accident of birth some lives are given great importance whilst others are completely expendable. I wanted to see the bizarre nature of royalty and its archaic sexism whereby princes are sent to war whilst princesses are dressed up in expensive clothes to receive bouquets of flowers and wave at crowds of admirers. Few of us have ever heard Kate Middleton speak and yet we see millions of photographs of her and read endless column inches about her outfits. I wanted to see through the eyes of the mermaids our obsession with a certain artificial, narrow idea of beauty, to see the power of the media to distort and shape our sense of self.

Tell us about the decision to involve teenage girls in the production.

Our production will involve a chorus of young women recruited in each city on tour who will create the sound of the mermaids singing. They will also take part in a nationwide project that accompanies the show that looks at the effect of the media on girls' sense of self and empowers them to challenge myths about femininity. Onstage the mermaid chorus will bear witness as a girl faces the challenge of becoming a young woman in a complex world.

The play begins very much in our contemporary world. There is
a sense of recession, of a family struggling to cope. Was it
important to you to enter the story through a modern teenager?

Yes, I wanted to avoid it feeling like a twee middle-class story
about a girl who reads fairy tales. At the beginning of the play we
see how a teenager is ostracised because she is still, at thirteen,
playing imaginary games. She lives by the sea and loves to swim
and is fascinated by mermaids, imagining that they exist and can
speak to her. I wanted to explore the pressure on young women to
grow up quickly and abandon play, becoming preoccupied by
appearance, judging one another and seeing one another as
competitors. Her father has been made redundant and so she can't
afford the branded products her classmates are wearing. Whilst
her erstwhile friends are all at a party having a makeover she sits
alone staring at the screen seeking escape. When instead a nasty
video message appears from her classmates she turns to her
favourite fairy story of *The Little Mermaid* for answers. Diving
down into the world of the story we watch her as real life starts to
entwine with that of the mermaids.

A Nick Hern Book

Mermaid first published in Great Britain in 2015 as a paperback original by Nick Hern Books Limited, The Glasshouse, 49a Goldhawk Road, London W12 8QP, in association with Shared Experience and Nottingham Playhouse

Mermaid copyright © 2015 Polly Teale

Polly Teale has asserted her moral right to be identified as the author of this work

Cover photograph: Kristin Perers

Designed and typeset by Nick Hern Books, London
Printed and bound by CPI Group (UK) Ltd, Croydon, CR0 4YY

A CIP catalogue record for this book is available from the British Library

ISBN 978 1 84842 486 9